THE PINEAPPLE COVE

COMPLETE SERIES COLLECTION

- POSEIDON'S STORM BLASTER
- A MERMAID'S PROMISE
- KING OF THE SEA
- PROTECTOR'S PLEDGE

By **Marina J. Bowman**

Illustrated by **Nathan Monção**

This is a work of fiction. Names, characters, places, and incidents either are the product of the author's imagination or are used fictitiously. Any resemblance to actual persons, locales, or events, living or dead, is coincidental.

Copyright © 2022 by Code Pineapple

All rights reserved. No part of this book may be reproduced or used in any manner without written permission of the copyright owner except for the use of quotations in a book review.

First paperback edition April 2022

Poseidon's Storm Blaster
Written by Marina J. Bowman
Illustrated by Nathan Monção

A Mermaid's Promise
Written by Marina J. Bowman
Illustrated by Nathan Monção

King of the Sea
Written by Marina J. Bowman
Illustrated by Nathan Monção

Protector's Pledge
Written by Marina J. Bowman
Illustrated by Nathan Monção

ISBN 978-1-950341-55-9 (paperback color)
ISBN 978-1-950341-56-6 (paperback black & white)
ISBN 978-1-950341-57-3 (ebook)

Published by Code Pineapple
www.codepineapple.com

DOWNLOAD THE AUDIOBOOK FREE!

READ THIS FIRST

Just to say thanks for getting my book, I'd like to give you the Audiobook version 100% FREE!

GET IT HERE:

thelegendofpineapplecove.com/bundle

ALSO BY MARINA J. BOWMAN

SCAREDY BAT

A supernatural detective series for kids with courage, teamwork, and problem solving. If you like solving mysteries and overcoming fears, you'll love this enchanting tale!

#1 Scaredy Bat and the Frozen Vampires
#2 Scaredy Bat and the Sunscreen Snatcher
#3 Scaredy Bat and the Missing Jellyfish
#4 Scaredy Bat and the Haunted Movie Set
#5 Scaredy Bat and the Mega Park Mystery

THE LEGEND OF PINEAPPLE COVE

A fantasy-adventure series for kids with bravery, kindness, and friendship. If you like reimagined mythology and animal sidekicks, you'll love this legendary story!

#1 Poseidon's Storm Blaster
#2 A Mermaid's Promise
#3 King of the Sea
#4 Protector's Pledge

*For all you brave adventurers,
explorers, and protectors*

DELPHI

CAPTAIN HOBBS

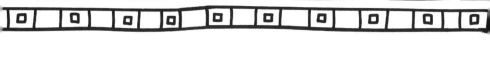

AUNT CORA

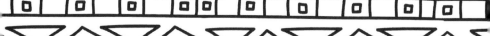

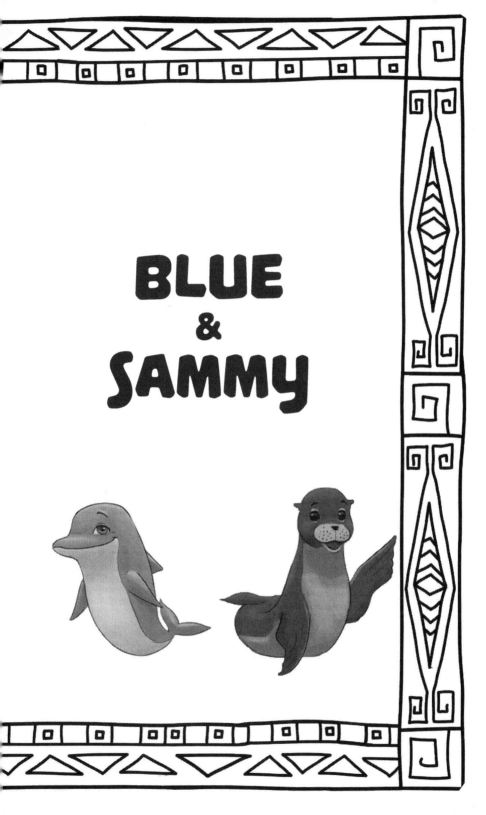

HIDDEN PINEAPPLE GAME

While you read, keep an eye out for hidden pineapples in the illustrations. When you're finished, you can check the answer key at the back of the book!

There is a place not far from here
Where big adventures await.
It's a town of magic and monsters and secrets
On an island, in the middle of the salty sea.

Pineapple Cove is its name.
The spot where it all begins.

There, kids can be explorers
And ride ships
And follow tattered, dark maps
And become the heroes
They were always meant to be.

THE LEGEND OF PINEAPPLE COVE

POSEIDON'S STORM BLASTER

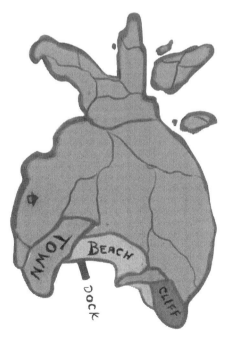

By **Marina J. Bowman**

Illustrated by **Nathan Monção**

CONTENTS

1. Unlikely Friends • 1
2. Gift From the Sea • 6
3. The Message • 12
4. Time to Prepare • 16
5. Aunt Cora's House • 22
6. A Reckless Mistake • 30
7. The Mysterious Red X • 34
8. The Guardians of Poseidon's Temple • 43
9. From the Oceans Cold and Warm • 50
10. The Monster • 57
11. Junior Protectors of Pineapple Cove • 65

EXTRAS

 Pineapple Answer Key • 69

 More LoPC • 70

CHAPTER 1

UNLIKELY FRIENDS

Kai was out on the beach that morning, collecting clams. They were salty and delicious, but Kai didn't like collecting them. It was hard work.

First, he would look for dimples in the sand. Then he'd dig and dig and dig until he found the clam. Finally, he'd fill the hole back up with sand. His dad was a fisherman, and that meant Kai went clamming *a lot*.

"Bor-ing," Kai sighed, and plopped another clam in his bright red bucket.

The sand was buttery yellow. The wind was soft and the waves were gentle. It was a beautiful day just like any other. It was Pineapple Cove after all.

"Shoot." Kai had broken another shell. He had a bad habit of hitting the clams with his shovel and cracking them. His dad was always telling him to slow down and be more careful, especially since he had turned ten.

As Kai bent to collect the clam, shouts and laughter rang out across the beach. A group of school kids darted across the beach, joking and kicking up sand.

"Hey!" said Alana, the girl at the front. "There's Kai!" The kids skidded to a halt in front of him, with big grins on their faces.

At least someone's having fun today, Kai thought.

"Hey, Kai," Alana said, flicking back her long, dark hair. "Are you coming to the games tonight? Everyone's going."

He'd forgotten about that! There was an event in the town hall that night, and everyone would be there for the start of summer break. "Sure!" he said, but the kids were already off again, running across the sand.

Kai sighed. He would have given anything to run off with them and leave his bucket of clams behind.

The kids slowed a little up ahead. They stopped. They pointed. They laughed. Kai looked up and squinted, trying to see what they'd found. *Oh, it's Delphi,* he realized.

Delphi was different. She had washed up onshore when she was little. Her only family was her adoptive Aunt Cora. The other townspeople thought Aunt Cora was odd. There were rumors that she had a house full of strange creatures.

The other kids thought Delphi was weird too. She never went in the water. She kept to herself. And she spent all her time with a blubbery sea lion named Sammy.

Right now, Delphi stood on top of a blue bucket with Sammy the sea lion next to her. She spoke to him like he could actually speak back, which was impossible of course.

The other kids laughed and shouted something at her. Delphi's face went red all over, like a big tomato. Finally, they ran off and left her alone.

Delphi fished around in her pocket and brought out some stones, her face shining and angry.

Kai frowned. He picked up his shovel and bucket and walked over to her. "Hey," he called out, "are you OK?"

Delphi didn't answer. Instead, she pulled back her arm and launched a glittering stone into the ocean. "Take that! And that!"

Kai stopped next to her. "Delphi?"

"What?" She said, continuing to throw stones. Sammy made a strange, throaty barking noise next to her. "No, I don't think so, Sammy."

"Um, I saw that the other kids were laughing and pointing at you."

"And you want to laugh and point too?" Delphi asked, tossing another stone. Sammy sniffed Kai's bucket of clams and licked his lips.

"No! I just wanted to check that you were OK."

Before Delphi could answer, a soft cry came from the ocean.

"What was that?" Kai and Delphi asked at the same time. Sammy whimpered and flopped backward on his flippers, hiding behind Delphi.

CHAPTER 2
GIFT FROM THE SEA

The sound came from the direction of a stone archway jutting out of the water. Kai sometimes fished near it with his father.

Delphi squinted at the sea and pointed. "There! It's a baby dolphin! It sounds like it's in trouble!"

Kai dropped his bucket of clams. "We've got to help it. Come on!"

But Delphi didn't move. "I c-can't. I can't go in the water."

"Then I'll go." Kai waded through the water. He crashed into the waves, and the waves crashed into him. Kai was a great swimmer.

Kai reached the dolphin in no time. It had

sleek, bluish-gray skin. A net was hooked over its long nose. Kai gently placed his hand on the dolphin. "Hey, it's OK, Blue. Can I call you that? You'll be OK."

Kai bobbed in the salt water and untied the net. The dolphin squeaked in relief and dove into the water. It was free!

As Kai swam back to shore, the dolphin popped up next to him. This time it had something shiny in its mouth.

"What do you have, Blue?" Kai opened his hand, and Blue dropped the item in his palm.

Kai gasped. It was a gold trident necklace!

Blue chirp-clicked, did a happy little flip, and disappeared beneath the waves. Kai swam back to the beach and rejoined Delphi.

"That was brave of you, Kai." Delphi wiggled her toes atop the bucket. "I'm sorry I didn't help. I'm...afraid of the water. I have been for a long time."

"It's OK. Why are you afraid of the water?" Kai asked.

Delphi twisted her fingers through the rope around her waist. "I'm sure you already know, but…I washed up on shore when I was little. I don't remember much, but every time I go near water I get a bit…itchy. And scared. I can't swim…or I could and I don't remember." Delphi shook her head. "It doesn't matter. What's that in your hand?"

"Oh, yeah!" Kai showed Delphi the trident necklace and told her what had happened.

"It's a gift from the sea. You should put it on!" Delphi smiled, opening her arms wide. Sammy barked in agreement.

Kai's fingers tingled as he lifted the necklace. A gust of wind ruffled his hair, and the sun, which had disappeared behind some clouds, reappeared. A circle of light fell around Kai. He slipped the trident necklace over his head. It was heavier than he expected, and warm against his wet skin.

"Wow," Delphi said, standing on tiptoe on her bucket. "I wonder how the dolphin found it. Or where it came from."

"I don't know, but it's pretty cool."

"You can say that again."

"It's pretty—"

BONG-BONG-BONG! A bell clanged three times, loud and clear, from the town square.

"What's going on? Three bells are for emergencies, right?" Delphi asked.

"We'd better go find out," Kai said.

Together they ran back to their town, with Sammy flippering along close behind.

CHAPTER 3
THE MESSAGE

Kai and Delphi hurried into Pineapple Cove. They ran past the baker's shop, where smells of yummy fresh bread drifted out. They ran past the coffee shop and the florist's, but everything was quiet.

Finally, they rushed into the town square. There was a crowd of a hundred people gathered in front of the town hall. On the stage, right at the front of it, stood the mayor.

He held a piece of crinkly parchment in his hand. Carl, the messenger pelican, was perched awkwardly on his shoulder. The mayor cleared his throat, and Carl ruffled his pinky-white feathers. "Carl has just delivered this message from one of the ships out at sea."

Kai moved closer to the stage. His dad's fishing ship was out at sea.

"Dear Mayor," the mayor read, while Carl pecked at the mayor's hair. "Something terrible has happened, and we are writing this letter to warn the people of Pineapple Cove."

Whispers rushed through the crowd.

The mayor continued reading. "It was a normal morning. All our poles were out over the side of the boat. We had just caught a gigantic fish, and then…it happened."

"What happened?" someone called out.

"The ship started rocking from one side to the other." The mayor's eyes were round as coconuts now. "And then there was a big *CRASH*."

Carl ruffled his feathers, slip-sliding on the mayor's fancy jacket.

The mayor read further. "A giant octopus monster attacked our ship! Its tentacles crushed

our mast, and it ate our fish."

"Oh no!" someone yelled. A man in the crowd fainted.

The mayor continued. "We were able to escape from the ship on one of the lifeboats."

A sigh of relief swept through the crowd. Kai relaxed a little – his dad was safe. But a giant octopus monster?

The mayor raised his hand and quieted everyone. "But now the monster is headed directly for Pineapple Cove!" The mayor stopped reading. He looked around at the crowd.

"This is terrible!" someone yelled.

"What are we going to do?" someone else asked.

"Everyone calm down," the mayor said, as he tried to push Carl off his shoulder. But the panicked shouting continued.

Kai and Delphi hurried through the crowd, their stomachs squiggled up with fear. Sammy the sea lion flopped along behind them, barking all the way.

CHAPTER 4

TIME TO PREPARE

Kai was determined to find his mom and younger sister. Delphi needed to find her aunt. They ran through the crowd, past the panicking adults.

"Why is this happening?" the baker shouted.

"What can we do against a sea monster?" the florist asked.

"My house is right on the water!" the coffee shop owner yelled.

"*All* our houses are on the water!" the baker responded.

"We need to come up with a plan," a woman said, calmly. That was Kai's mom! He ran over to her and gave her a big hug. She had Kai's

younger sister, Maya, with her. Delphi's Aunt Cora stood beside them, clutching her seaweed purse.

On the stage, the mayor cleared his throat. He held out his hands. "Everyone calm down, please."

Next to Kai, Aunt Cora shifted and cast a glance in his direction. Her eyes twinkled, and her gaze fixed on his trident necklace. There

was a gasp as Aunt Cora ran and jumped on stage next to the mayor.

"We need Captain Hobbs!" Aunt Cora shouted, waving her arms. "He's the Protector for Pineapple Cove. He can help us with the sea monster."

A few of the kids nearby rolled their eyes. Alana, who had been on the beach that morning, sniggered at Delphi.

"Hobbs won't help us. He turned his back on us long ago," a man muttered.

"Yeah, I haven't seen him around in ages," a woman said.

The mayor guided Aunt Cora off the stage. "Everyone must go home and prepare for the attack as best as possible," he said. "That's all we can do right now."

"When will it come?" Kai's mom asked.

"The fishing ship was less than a day away when it was attacked," the mayor replied, glancing at the crinkly paper again. "We must be ready, right away."

More shouts broke out, but Kai had stopped listening. A wave of heat rushed through him.

He wanted to find the sea monster himself. To protect his village. To get even with the sea monster for attacking his dad's boat. He looked over at his mom and sister and calmed down a little. No, he should stay and help protect the house. What could he do against a sea monster, anyway?

The kids from school rushed past, but a few of them slowed. "Delphi, you're so weird. And your aunt is too. Do you really think some lame captain will help us?" Alana said.

"Don't talk about my aunt like that," Delphi said, folding her arms. "You might not believe her, but I do."

"What do you think, Kai?" Alana asked.

Kai froze. Sammy the sea lion gave an encouraging bark. "I – um –" He didn't want to lie, but he didn't want to hurt Delphi's feelings either.

"Oh, whatever. Come on, guys," Alana said and ran off with the others, still laughing at what Aunt Cora had said.

"You don't believe my aunt?" Delphi asked Kai, a big frown wrinkling up her olive forehead.

"It's not that I don't believe her. It's just that I need to make sure my house is protected in case the monster attacks. You heard the mayor. It could come at any moment."

"Fine," Delphi said. A heavy silence hung between them.

Finally, Kai's mom and Aunt Cora rejoined them and broke the silence.

"Kai, it's time to go home and prepare the house." Kai's mom looked from Kai to Delphi and back again. "And once we're finished, why don't you go help Delphi with her house? What do you think, Cora?"

Aunt Cora smiled mischievously. "That would be lovely."

Kai eyed Delphi, but she was staring at the ground. "OK, sure."

"Wonderful," Kai's mom said. "Let's get to it."

Kai followed his mom and Maya to their house, and Delphi followed Aunt Cora to their house. It was time to prepare for the sea monster attack.

CHAPTER 5
AUNT CORA'S HOUSE

Kai made quick work of preparing his family's house. They closed up shutters, and he helped his mom place wood planks over the doors. They packed away anything that could get broken or tossed around in the house.

As soon as they were done, Kai set off to Aunt Cora's house to do the same for her. Aunt Cora's house was weathered – a brick home with a front porch and a seashell stepping stone path.

The speckled front door opened, and Aunt Cora stepped out. She held a large iguana the length of her arm. "Hello, Kai," she said.

"Come inside and have something to eat. You must be hungry after all that work at your house." There was still that strange twinkle in her eye.

Kai followed Aunt Cora inside, his heart beating a little faster than usual. He stopped inside the doorway. He could barely believe his eyes.

The inside of Aunt Cora's house was filled with nests and habitats, each one with a different creature inside. There were ancient turtles and glowing frogs. There was a tank with a beautiful blue fish inside. There was a bubbling tube in the center of the room, filled with seaweed and starfish. There were birds with sharp beaks and necks that were too long. There was a curious monkey sitting on top of a perch in the corner.

Sammy the sea lion barked and flip-flopped over to a big circular pool next to a set of wooden stairs. He dived into it and splashed water everywhere.

"Whoa," Kai said, shaking his head. He had never seen so many creatures in one place before.

Aunt Cora laughed and came closer. She tapped on the bubbling tube. A strange fish, with eyes that were far too bright and smart, swooshed into view and flapped a fin at them. It smiled, or so it seemed, and revealed a mouth full of wickedly sharp teeth.

"This is Finley," she said. "Say 'hello,' Finley." Finley the fish waved his tail at them.

"He-hello," Kai stammered.

"Don't be scared, Kai. All the creatures here are safe," Aunt Cora said. Kai relaxed and moved closer to Finley's tank.

"Well, as long as they're not hungry," Aunt

Cora added. "And come to think of it, Finley's always hungry, so make sure not to stick your fingers in his tank." Finley smiled. Kai gulped.

Aunt Cora motioned to Kai. He followed her and entered a small dining room with shining seashell counters, a table, and four mismatched chairs. Delphi was at the table, paging through a book called *Creatures of the Deep*.

Kai sat down across from Delphi while Aunt Cora prepared them lunch in the kitchen.

"Hey," Kai said. Delphi looked up, then went back to flipping through the book.

Kai tried again, lowering his voice. "I'm sorry about earlier…with Alana and the other kids. I don't think your aunt is crazy. I just don't know about this Captain Hobbs."

Delphi looked up again and stared at Kai. Finally, she nodded and said, "Thanks."

"For what?" Kai asked.

"None of the other kids have ever apologized to me. Or been nice to me." Delphi smiled. Kai smiled back.

The smell of grilled fish and chips drifted through the room. Kai's stomach growled.

"I'm starving," Kai said.

"Meeee too," Delphi agreed.

"Me three!" Aunt Cora said as she walked over. She set down plates of delicious fish and chips in front of them. Kai and Delphi thanked Aunt Cora and dug into their food.

"Guess what happened to us today, Aunt Cora?" Delphi said with a mouthful of chips.

"What is it, my starfish?"

"Kai saved a dolphin from a fishing net today!"

"Ah! So that's where you got the trident necklace from," Aunt Cora said.

"Wait. How did you know that?" Kai asked.

Aunt Cora didn't answer. She bustled out of the room, her footsteps clunking on the stone floor. She was back in no time, carrying a leatherbound book. She plopped it down in the middle of the table and opened it up.

She pointed to a sketch of a man with a grizzly beard and a captain's hat. Around his neck hung a…

"Trident necklace!" Kai exclaimed.

"This is Captain Hobbs," Aunt Cora said. "He was a Protector of Pineapple Cove for the longest time. Actually, he was one of Poseidon's Protectors of the Seventh Sea. Pineapple Cove was the home base for all of the Protectors."

Aunt Cora smiled. "I still remember when he first came back to town, carrying a sack full of crystals from one of his adventures. Whenever there was trouble in town, he was there to help." The smile on her face faded. "Until one day…"

"What happened?" Kai asked.

"I'm not sure exactly. All I know is that he disappeared when the town needed him most. Then he turned up at the Broken Barrel Pub several months later and has been there ever since."

"Do you think the necklace is connected to these Protectors?" Delphi asked.

"It might be," Aunt Cora said mysteriously.

So many questions filled Kai's head at once. *What does a Protector do? And how do*

you become one? What happened to Captain Hobbs? The captain seemed to be the key. He might even help them defeat the sea monster.

"Where is the Broken Barrel Pub?" Kai asked. "Just curious."

Aunt Cora raised an eyebrow. "It's right off the trade route, two nautical miles southeast of here. Not far at all."

That settles it, Kai thought. He would go find the captain and bring him to Pineapple Cove. His stomach went floopsy with excitement.

Delphi eyed Kai suspiciously. Kai cleared his throat. "So how can I help with preparing the house?"

Aunt Cora smiled. "We've done just about everything we can do to prepare. But thank you for your kind offer, dear."

Kai wolfed down the rest of his lunch. "I should head home. My mom will be expecting me soon." Kai thanked Aunt Cora and said goodbye to her and Delphi. But Kai didn't head home. Instead he hurried toward the dock, where his dad kept their small sailboat.

CHAPTER 6
A RECKLESS MISTAKE

Just as Kai was about to push the boat into the water, a bark sounded behind him.

"Wait!" Delphi jogged up to him and Sammy flopped next to her. "You can't go find Captain Hobbs by yourself. You need to make a plan first."

"Sure I can," Kai said. "I know where he is and how to get there."

"But...did you plan a route? Do you know what you're going to say if you find him?" Delphi asked.

"I'll figure it out," Kai said as the bow of the boat slid into the water. "And if you're so worried, you should come along with me."

Delphi looked at the waves bumping up against the boat. "Um…are you a good sailor? I-is it safe?"

Kai put his hands on his hips. "I'm the best. It's perfectly safe."

"OK. I guess it's fine as long as I don't have to touch the water." Delphi turned and ran up the beach.

"Huh? Where is she going?" Kai scratched his head. Sammy barked, sharing his confusion.

Delphi reappeared, and Kai coughed to keep from laughing. "What are you wearing?"

Delphi had put about twenty floaty devices on her arms and legs. She handed one to Kai. "Just in case," she said.

Delphi moved toward the boat carefully, and Kai helped her inside. Sammy splashed in after her. Delphi settled in and tucked her bag against her side. "Let's go!" she cried.

Kai pushed the boat all the way into the water and hopped inside. The sail puffed out, and they moved steadily away from shore.

"So how are we going to get to the Broken Barrel Pub?" Delphi asked. The boat continued to float away from the beach.

"Easy, I just have to use the stars. My dad taught me how…oh, wait. There are no stars out yet." Kai's shoulders slumped. They drifted further away from land. He looked at Delphi, expecting her to freak out.

"I'm sorry, I guess I should have thought things through more. I'll turn us around," Kai said. He started to adjust the sails.

"Well, can we use this?" Delphi pulled out a round object from her bag.

Kai looked in Delphi's hands. "A compass! Yes! We can use that." Kai exhaled. Delphi handed him the compass.

Kai studied the compass. "Thanks! You were right, planning was a good idea." He turned the boat to face southeast.

Delphi's cheeks turned pink. "You're welcome. Do you want to talk about what we should say when we find Captain Hobbs?"

"Yeah, let's do it," Kai said.

While the two bounced around ideas, Kai made sure they sailed in the right direction. Delphi made sure the water stayed put. And Sammy made sure they had fishy snacks for their journey.

CHAPTER 7

THE MYSTERIOUS RED X

Kai and Delphi approached the tiniest island they'd ever seen. In fact, it was more of a large rock sticking out of the water. On top of the rock sat an enormous teetering ship.

At last, they rocked up against a barrel jetty, and Kai helped Delphi out of the boat. A long line of barrels strung together led right up to the ship.

"The Broken Barrel looks just like a broken old ship," Kai said, "but with a door." A rumbling noise nearby made Kai jump. "What's that?"

Delphi giggled and put a finger to her lips.

She pointed to Sammy, who was curled up in the bottom of their boat, snoring peacefully.

"You know, this ship used to carry Piña Pop along the Ananas trade route. But then it crashed into this tiny island, and it's been stuck here ever since," Delphi whispered as they tied their little boat to a barrel.

"Yeah, my dad told me the Broken Barrel is a popular place for fishermen to stop for food and drinks," Kai said.

They set off across the barrels, hopping from one to the other, their flip-flops squidging against the sun-baked wood.

As they got closer, the noises of people singing and laughing reached their ears. They hopped off the last barrel and entered the pub with a creak of its moldy wooden door.

The sights, sounds, and smells of the Broken Barrel hit them right away. The pub was filled with sailors and seafarers of all kinds. Kai and Delphi scanned the room, looking for Captain Hobbs.

A large man had his head on the table and looked like he was taking an afternoon nap. A small man performed a card trick. A group of men and women had their arms linked together and sang a merry song. The smell of Piña Pop filled Kai and Delphi's noses. A lady with an eye patch cleaned glasses behind the bar. Kai guessed that she was the captain of the Broken Barrel.

At last they spotted someone familiar, sitting in the corner with his head down. The man barely looked like the one from Aunt Cora's drawing. He had wrinkles under his eyes and much of his face was hidden behind a grizzly gray beard and a hat.

Kai and Delphi approached him. "Captain Hobbs? Is that you?" Kai asked.

"Who's asking?" Captain Hobbs grumbled.

"I'm Kai, and this is Delphi. Pineapple Cove is in danger. We need your help."

"I can't help you," Captain Hobbs grumbled again. He didn't even look up at them.

"Come on, Captain," Delphi said, folding her arms. "We know you're the Protector for Pineapple Cove. A sea monster is coming. You have to help."

The captain sighed. "I used to be. But then I made an unforgivable mistake."

"What mistake? What happened?" Kai asked.

"Terrible, terrible mistake," the captain repeated.

Kai wouldn't give up. "If you can't help us yourself, please tell us how to defeat the monster."

"It's impossible. The answer you seek is locked away. And to find the key, you must perform a selfless act of bravery. Only then will the trident key appear."

Kai and Delphi looked at each other. "You mean like this?" Kai held out the sparkling trident necklace.

Finally, the captain raised his head. His eyes were blue and bright. He stared at the necklace in stunned silence. "How...where did you get that?"

Hope returned to the captain's face. He touched his finger to the trident and said, "I think I may be able to help you after all."

"You can?" Delphi grinned. "I knew it!"

"Kai saved a dolphin from a fishing net. Then the dolphin gave him the necklace!" Delphi put her hands on her hips.

Hobbs glanced around the crowded bar and leaned forward. Kai and Delphi moved closer to his table. "Pineapple Cove has a secret."

"What's the secret?" asked Kai.

"Pineapple Cove is home to a magic portal that leads to Poseidon's temple. Inside the temple is an ancient artifact infused with the power of the king of the sea himself. The artifact is called Poseidon's Storm Blaster."

Hobbs reached into his pocket and pulled out a wrinkled old map. "Here." He pressed his finger to a big red X. "This is where the portal is located."

Kai stared at the X. "Hey, this is near where my dad takes me fishing."

Hobbs nodded. "This is where you need to go. Once you have the Storm Blaster, you can defeat the sea monster."

Kai looked at Delphi and remembered his mistake with the compass. He wasn't sure he was the right person for this mission.

"Captain, maybe *you* should have the trident necklace. You can use it to get the Storm Blaster and protect Pineapple Cove." Kai lifted the necklace off his neck and offered it to Hobbs.

Captain Hobbs shook his head. "No, the necklace is yours. It was sent to you because of your selfless act. It means you've been invited to become a Junior Protector. I believe you are meant for this task."

"And so do I!" Delphi exclaimed.

"OK." Kai nodded to Delphi. This might be their only chance to save Pineapple Cove.

They had to do it. "Let's go!" Kai pointed to the door and lifted the map.

Kai and Delphi started to walk off, but Captain Hobbs' chair scraped the floor. "Wait," he said. "I will come with you. This mission may not be mine, but I can still help. Pineapple Cove was once my home too."

Together, Hobbs, Kai, Delphi, and Sammy boarded the captain's ship. They set sail toward Pineapple Cove, in search of the mysterious red X.

CHAPTER 8

THE GUARDIANS OF POSEIDON'S TEMPLE

In no time at all, they reached the location of the magic portal.

"We have arrived," said Hobbs triumphantly.

"It's here?" Kai asked, as they sailed toward the stone archway, just off Pineapple Cove's coast. Delphi sat on the side of the boat now, and actually dipped a finger into the water.

"It's not so bad," she muttered. A bit of it splashed on her arm and she let out a little cry. She laughed.

Captain Hobbs nodded. "Yes, this is the portal."

Kai didn't understand. This was the same old rock archway that everyone knew about. In fact, Kai had sailed underneath it before with his father.

How could it be a magical opening to Poseidon's Island?

"Come, Kai," Hobbs said, nudging him forward. "Go to the front of the boat, hold your trident necklace, and say, 'By Poseidon's invitation, let me pass.'"

The captain didn't seem like one to make jokes, so Kai did as he was told. He hurried to the front of the boat, squishing past Delphi. They sailed toward the rock archway. Sammy covered his eyes with a moist flipper.

"By Poseidon's invitation," Kai said, holding out his necklace. "Let me pass."

There was a shimmery flash. The space under the archway turned purplish-blue and transparent. The boat sailed through it and out the other side.

An island that surely hadn't been there a moment before appeared in front of them.

Captain Hobbs sailed up to it and stopped the boat. He let down a wooden plank onto the sand. "This is Poseidon's Island," Captain Hobbs said. "I must wait with the ship. You two get the Storm Blaster."

Kai and Delphi slid down the plank together. Sammy followed them. Delphi didn't cry even once, though she still had her floatation devices on. She even waded through the shallow water on the beach to get to the sand.

"Look over there." Delphi pointed to a temple ahead of them.

Squiggly pictures were scratched on the outside. The dark entrance glowed a soft blue.

"Here we go," Kai said. Delphi followed him, stripping off the floaties as she walked. They stopped in front of the entrance.

The temple was dark, and they couldn't see what was inside. Strange echoes floated out to them. Kai and Delphi each took a deep breath and stepped forward.

The inside of the temple was lit by blue orbs that hung from the ceiling by strips of seaweed. Statues of people with tridents lined the walls.

They walked on and found a massive doorway inside the temple. On either side of the glittering bronze doors stood two blue people. Royal blue from head to toe. They had pointy ears and webbed fingers. They wore stern expressions and held spears in their hands.

"We are the guardians of Poseidon's temple. What is your purpose here?" one of the guards asked, pointing the spear at Kai.

Kai cleared his throat. "I am Kai of Pineapple Cove. We're here for the Storm Blaster," he said. "Our town is in danger from a horrible octopus monster."

The two guards looked at each other. The blue woman on the left wrinkled up her nose. "I see you possess the trident necklace. That means you are pure of heart."

The other guard nodded. "You may enter."

"That's it? You'll let us pass, just like that?" Delphi asked. Sammy barked and flipped up to her side.

"Only Kai may enter, as he possesses the trident necklace," the guards said.

Delphi frowned and looked down at the floor.

Kai stepped forward. "She's with me. I wouldn't be here if it weren't for her. Please let Delphi and Sammy come too."

The guards stared at them for a while and then finally stepped back. The blue woman opened the doors to the room.

It was dark in there. Scary, even. Kai wasn't afraid of much, but the temple was seriously creepy.

Could they really do this? Delphi nodded toward the room.

Kai nodded back at Delphi, and they walked through the doorway together.

The doors slammed shut behind them. They were plunged into darkness. Sammy gave a little whine at their side.

CHAPTER 9

FROM THE OCEANS COLD AND WARM

Up ahead, on a pedestal in a circle of light, sat a crystal case. Inside the crystal case was the Storm Blaster.

"There it is," Kai whispered, holding his trident necklace.

"How do we get to it?" asked Delphi. Water surrounded the pedestal, and there were no steps across.

Kai started forward, ready to jump into the water and swim across, but then he stopped. He looked back at Delphi, remembering what happened when he didn't think things through before.

Kai crouched at the edge of the water. He dipped his finger into the pool and swirled it around. The water bubbled and churned. Kai jumped back. Dozens of bright eyes and sharp teeth appeared in the water.

"It's a whole family of Finleys!" gasped Delphi. "But bigger!"

"What do we do?" Kai asked, backing away from the water.

Sammy barked next to Kai, and he looked around, frowning.

The sea lion chewed on the rope around Delphi's waist. "Sammy, this is serious, and all you can think about is snack time?"

Sammy barked twice and nudged the rope again. "Oh! The rope! We can use it to get the Storm Blaster!" Delphi said.

Delphi quickly untied the rope from her waist. She made a lasso out of it and tossed it toward the ceiling. It fell back down with a thud. She tossed it up again, and it fell to the floor again. She threw it harder and pulled, roping one of the hanging blue orbs.

"Ah ha!" Delphi yelled. She offered the rope to Kai. "Here, you can swing across to the pedestal using this rope. Unlock the glass case with the trident key. Then swing back across on the rope. Easy-peasy."

Kai looked at the rope. "Are you sure that will work?"

Delphi gave a little tug on the rope. "Almost positive."

"OK, I'll do it." Kai took the rope from Delphi and faced the water. He ran and jumped, swinging toward the pedestal. The Finleys jumped out of the water and snapped at Kai's ankles, just missing him. He landed on the pedestal. Delphi and Sammy cheered.

Kai stepped up to the crystal case. A lock sat on top of it with three prongs. Kai placed his trident necklace in it. There was a click-hiss, and the case's lid slid open.

The Storm Blaster glistened inside, hovering in mid-air. Carefully, Kai removed it. He tucked the Blaster under one arm and grabbed the rope with both hands. He swung back across. Kai had almost made it to the other side when he felt the Storm Blaster slipping. It slipped down and down until...*splash*! It fell into the water below.

"Oh no!" Kai yelled.

Delphi ran to the water's edge and bent down. "Bad Finley!" she said, as she swatted one of the fish away. She grabbed the Storm Blaster before it sank to the bottom.

Kai landed next to Delphi and pulled her back from the hungry fish. His heart thumped inside his chest.

Delphi finally caught her breath. "See, easy-peasy." She and Kai laughed. Delphi handed the blaster back to Kai.

The doors to the room swung open, and the two blue guardians stepped through. They slammed their spears down once. "Well done," said the blue man, pointing to the glass case. "You have outsmarted our man-eating fish and retrieved the Storm Blaster."

He pointed to the blaster in Kai's hands. "The Storm Blaster holds the power of the sea. With it you can calm any water-loving creature.

It can be shared with others who are worthy."

The blue woman nodded and said, "To activate the Storm Blaster, you must say…"

'From the oceans cold and warm,

I summon Poseidon's storm.'

"Do you understand?"

"I think so. Thank you," Kai said to the blue guardians.

"C'mon, Kai!" Delphi tugged on his arm. "We have to get back to the boat and through the portal before it's too late!"

CHAPTER 10
THE MONSTER

Delphi, Kai, Sammy, and Captain Hobbs sailed back through the portal, quick as they could. The sun was just dipping down in the sky. The water was calm. Pineapple Cove's beaches were peaceful.

"We're here!" Delphi held onto the railing. "And everything is fine. I don't see any monsters."

Kai grinned at her. "You seem more comfortable near the water now."

"Yeah, I'm starting to get used to it. I have to, or else I'll miss out on everything," Delphi said.

Suddenly the boat rocked to the right. It rocked to the left. The wood groaned, and then…*BOOM!*

Kai rushed to the railing. He leaned over and looked down into the deep blue sea.

"Oh no!" Kai yelled.

A giant octopus monster bashed the side of the boat with its tentacles. *Boom-boom-bash.*

Kai wobbled. He hugged the Storm Blaster to his chest. He tipped forward and…*SPLASH*!

"Kai!" Delphi gasped. Kai banged his head on the side of the ship and started to sink.

Captain Hobbs stood at the wheel. He twisted it this way and that. "Delphi! I have to steer us away from the monster."

"But Kai fell in!" Delphi shouted. And I can't go in the water, she thought.

But she had to do something. She untied the rope from around her waist again and made a lasso. She tried to loop it around Kai, but he was completely under the water now.

Delphi looked down at her sea lion friend. "Sammy, quick! Dive in and save Kai!"

But Sammy shook his head. He was afraid of the octopus monster. There was nothing else to do. Delphi was still afraid of the water, but she couldn't let anything happen to Kai.

Delphi took a deep breath and climbed over the railing.

She counted, "One, two, three!"

She dove into the water. It was icy cold.

Delphi kicked her legs. She splashed her arms. She opened her eyes and she swam. *I'm doing it! I'm swimming!*

Delphi found Kai sinking down toward the bottom of the ocean. His eyes were closed.

She grabbed him. There was another splash, and Sammy appeared. He grabbed Delphi's arm in his mouth and pulled on it. He dragged Delphi and Kai to the surface.

Delphi patted Kai on the cheeks. "Wake up!"

Kai choked and spluttered. "Delphi, you're in the water!"

"I know!" There wasn't much time to talk. The sea monster had spotted them. It gave a horrible roar and detached from the boat. It squelched toward them.

Kai and Delphi grabbed onto Sammy, and he swam them to the beach. "Thanks Sammy," Kai said, turning toward the octopus monster.

The monster was closer to shore now, ready to chomp them up. Its beaky mouth appeared, its tentacles flopping onto the beach. One landed right next to Kai's foot.

"Oh no you don't." Kai raised the Storm Blaster. "From the oceans cold and warm, I summon Poseidon's storm." The blaster glowed white and shook in Kai's hands.

Kai pumped the handle with all his might. A swirling stream shot out of the end of the blaster. And it hit the monster right in the face.

The sea monster stopped. It turned and blinked. It shook its tentacles. In fact, it looked as if it had just woken up from a Sunday afternoon nap.

Finally, it slothered off to sea.

"That cooled it off," Delphi joked.

Sammy gave a terrific bark. Kai grinned. Delphi laughed, pushing wet hair back from her forehead.

Cheers rang out from the town. The people of Pineapple Cove ran down the beach. Kai's mom and dad hugged him tightly. Aunt Cora wrapped her arms around Delphi.

Captain Hobbs came down from the boat. "It looks like Pineapple Cove has a new Junior Protector." He winked at Kai.

Aunt Cora put her hand on Hobbs' shoulder. "Welcome back, Captain." Hobbs tipped his hat at Cora.

The mayor walked up to Aunt Cora. "It seems you may have been right, Cora. Next time we'll have to listen to you more carefully." Carl the pelican bobbed his head in agreement.

"I appreciate that, Mr. Mayor," Aunt Cora said.

The fishermen from the lifeboat raised Kai and Delphi in the air.

"I wonder why the sea monster attacked. It looked like it was under a spell," Delphi said.

It didn't matter now. The monster was gone. And Kai would have the Storm Blaster if it came back.

Thanks to Kai's bold stand-off and Delphi's brave swim, Pineapple Cove was safe.

CHAPTER 11

JUNIOR PROTECTORS OF PINEAPPLE COVE

The following morning, everything was peaceful in Pineapple Cove. The waves washed against the butter-yellow shore. Delphi and Kai walked along the beach. Delphi held the bucket, and Kai worked the shovel. Together, they dug for clams and laughed at Sammy.

The sea lion splashed in and out of the water, barking every now and again.

"See, if we dig a hole *next to* where the clam is, we don't break as many shells."

Kai grinned. "Thanks for helping me. I'm going to need all the help I can get soon. Captain Hobbs is going to train me as a Junior Protector!"

"Wow. That's so cool," Delphi replied. "Well, I'll help you with clamming any time you want."

Kai was lucky to have Delphi as a friend, and he gave her another smile to show it. Sammy flippered around nearby, barking happily.

In the distance, a group of kids ran up to them, headed by Alana. Delphi stopped clamming and bit her bottom lip.

"Hi guys," Alana said, waving at them. "Are you coming to the games tonight? The mayor said we can do them now that the sea monster is gone."

Delphi and Kai exchanged a glance. "Sure," they said together.

Alana and the others rushed off again, chatting amongst themselves. For once, they didn't point or laugh at Delphi and Sammy.

"OK, so we can go to–" Kai started.

"What's that?" Delphi asked.

A clickety-chirp had interrupted them. They both looked out at the ocean.

"It's Blue!" Kai shouted. Blue the dolphin flipped out of the water and swam closer to shore. Kai and Delphi rushed out to meet her.

"What have you got there, Blue?" Delphi asked. The dolphin opened its mouth. Inside it was a purple trident necklace. Delphi gasped and took it from the dolphin. "For me?" she asked.

"You deserve it," Kai replied. "You saved the Storm Blaster from the Finleys. And you jumped into the water to save me." Delphi slipped the necklace over her head. A gust of wind blew her hair and the sun shone brighter.

Together, they jogged back to shore and waved at Blue. The dolphin dove back into the ocean. Sammy chased after her, but gave up after a while and came back.

"Now I can train with Captain Hobbs too!" Delphi said, holding her necklace. "I wonder what else we don't know about this island."

"Yeah, I get the feeling that we're just beginning to discover its secrets." Kai and Delphi linked arms and walked back to the clam bucket together. They were Junior Protectors of Pineapple Cove.

HIDDEN PINEAPPLE ANSWER KEY

There are 14 pineapples hidden throughout the illustrations in this story. Did you spot them all?

CHAPTER 1 = 🍍
CHAPTER 2 = 🍍
CHAPTER 3 = 🍍 🍍
CHAPTER 4 = 🍍
CHAPTER 5 = 🍍
CHAPTER 6 = 🍍
CHAPTER 7 = 🍍 🍍
CHAPTER 8 = 🍍 🍍 🍍
CHAPTER 9 = NONE
CHAPTER 10 = 🍍 🍍
CHAPTER 11 = NONE

QUESTIONS FOR DISCUSSION

1. What did you enjoy about this book?
2. What are some of the major themes of this story?
3. How are Kai and Delphi similar? How are they different? How did they help each other in the story?
4. What doubts or fears did the characters express in the book? When have you been afraid? How have you dealt with your fears?
5. The Legend of Pineapple Cove Book #1 ends with some loose ends. What do you think will happen in the next book in the series?

For more Discussion Questions, visit
thelegendofpineapplecove.com/bundle

COLOR IN YOUR OWN JOURNEY!

DESIGN YOUR OWN TRIDENT NECKLACE!

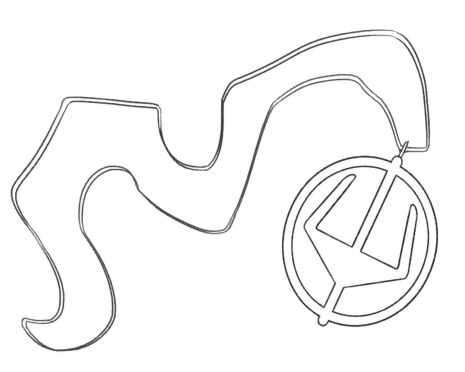

ADD YOUR OWN STYLE TO FINLEY AND FRIENDS!

For more coloring pages, visit:
thelegendofpineapplecove.com/bundle

The Legend of Pineapple Cove

A Mermaid's Promise

By **Marina J. Bowman**

Illustrated by **Nathan Monção**

CONTENTS

1. The Most Important Job • 81
2. Bang-Slurp-Squish-Slurp • 86
3. Race Against Slime • 92
4. Monster Misfire • 98
5. The Hidden Message • 104
6. I Have An Idea • 111
7. Sirenia Orbis • 118
8. An Unexpected Visitor • 126
9. The Collector • 135
10. A Trade of Jewels & Junk • 144
11. The Dancing Jelly • 152
12. Queen of Sirenia • 159
13. A Secret Revealed • 165
14. Salt Shakes & Promises • 172
15. The Captain Returns • 181

EXTRAS

 Pineapple Answer Key • 185
 More LoPC • 186

CHAPTER 1
THE MOST IMPORTANT JOB

"Oh, please, please, please can I come with you?" Maya hopped up and down in her seat at the breakfast table.

It was warm and sunny in Kai's house, and Delphi had joined the family for breakfast. Kai's mom had already put out plates for them on the wooden, creaky table. Eggs with runny yolks, sizzling bits of bacon, and delicious fried tomatoes were piled high on the table. He loved it all, and it was the perfect meal for this morning.

Kai and Delphi had their Protector training with Captain Hobbs today.

"Kai, please!" Maya slipped out of her

chair and squeezed between Delphi and Kai. "I know I'm strong enough."

"Sorry, Maya, but you're too young to be a Protector," Kai said.

Delphi nodded between bites of her eggs and bacon. "It can be dangerous. We do obstacle courses and practice cooling down monsters. It's an important job." She puffed out her chest.

Kai's mom sighed. "I hope you two won't give Captain Hobbs any trouble."

"We never give him trouble," Kai said, grinning.

"But sometimes trouble finds us," Delphi added, winking.

It was a joke Kai and Delphi shared, because they had definitely landed in a sticky situation not too long ago. But they had sent away a monster and saved Pineapple Cove. Now, Maya wanted to do the same thing.

"I can be strong," Maya said, lifting her arm. She made a muscle and tapped it. "See? And I can invent things to get rid of monsters!" Maya pointed to a jumble of fishing nets, coconut shells, and bird feathers in the corner of the room.

"Maya, of course you are brilliant and strong," Kai's mom said. "But you're still too young. Maybe when you're a little bit older you can join your brother."

"Hmph." Maya returned to her spot at the table and slumped down in her seat.

"Maya, I would love to see your inventions. Will you show me sometime?" Delphi asked.

"Okay." Maya gave Delphi a small smile.

Kai and Delphi finished off the last bits of their breakfast. Kai loved his sister, even though she could be annoying sometimes. He didn't want her to feel sad about him going off for the day and leaving her behind.

"Maya," he said as he took his plate to the sink. "You can't come with us, but you can do something even more important."

"What?" His sister bounced out of her chair and came over. "I'll do anything."

"You have to make sure you look after Mom while Dad is gone." Kai's dad was a fisherman and was out at sea at the moment. "And make sure that you help her around the house, too."

"That doesn't sound very important." Maya frowned.

"It's the most important job there is. Even more important than training to be a Protector." Kai put his hand on her shoulder. "Do you think you can do that?"

Maya's frown disappeared. Her expression grew serious, and she put her hand up against her forehead. "Yes, sir," she said, and saluted.

Kai gave his sister a quick hug, then did the same with his mom. "I'll be back later!"

"Thanks for breakfast!" said Delphi.

And with that, Kai and Delphi were out the door and on their way to their training.

CHAPTER 2

BANG-SLURP-SQUISH-SLURP

Kai and Delphi walked along the beach together, kicking up clumps of yellow sand. Waves licked their toes and drew back again, showing off pearly shells left behind. The weather was pleasantly warm, as usual.

They both wanted to be Poseidon's Protectors. They had been training almost every day that summer. They would practice their aim with toy water blasters, because the Storm Blaster had to be kept safe. They would do puzzles, and Captain Hobbs would teach them about the different types of sea life.

"I can't wait for training today," Delphi said, and dipped her toes in the cool ocean water. The waves rushed over her feet, and Delphi giggled. She was becoming more and more comfortable around water each day.

Sammy the Sea Lion hopped along beside them, barking, his flippers slapping and wet.

"Mm hmm." Kai shrugged.

"What's your favorite part of training?" Delphi asked, twirling her trident necklace.

"I like the obstacle course," Kai said, but he frowned.

"What's wrong?" Delphi asked. "Aren't you excited for training today?" They were on their way to meet Captain Hobbs at Aunt Cora's house. From there, they would head out to their super-secret training spot on the beach.

Kai sighed. "It's just... I already blasted a giant octopus monster, remember?"

"So?"

"So I don't need as much training. I already know how to use the Storm Blaster. It would be more fun to go out exploring and find some real monsters to blast."

"But it's still fun," Delphi said, as they turned onto the road that led out along the side of the town. The tar was already warm from the heat of the day. "It's nice to feel important. We're Junior Protectors in training. Besides, I like it better than spending all day at home, alone."

Delphi didn't like to be home alone. She didn't have many friends. Lots of the kids in Pineapple Cove thought Delphi was too "different."

"What about Sammy?" Kai asked.

The sea lion barked at Delphi, and she patted him on the head. "Of course, I'm never alone."

But Kai understood what she meant. Delphi had washed up on Pineapple Cove's beach when she was very little. Aunt Cora had adopted her, but Kai knew that Delphi sometimes wondered about where she had come from.

"Are you excited for tonight?" Delphi asked, grinning at him.

They had decided they would have a slumber party. Delphi's Aunt Cora had a house full of interesting sea creatures. Kai couldn't wait to play with them and to stay up late eating coco-nutty cookies.

"It's going to be the best," Kai said. "But what are we going to do?" Hopefully, Delphi wouldn't want to do more sea monster training.

"We can eat sweets. We can play games. And we can explore!"

"Explore?"

"Yeah, in the house. My aunt has a lot of hidden rooms and doors." Delphi rubbed her hands together. "Ooh! And we can tell scary stories."

Kai raised an eyebrow. "What kinds of scary stories?"

Delphi tapped her bottom lip. "Oh, I've got it." She lifted her thin, sticky-outie arms above her head and swirled them around. "And then… it came!"

"What did?" Kai looked at the road ahead.

"The sea monster from the deep, blue ocean."

"Again?" Kai laughed.

"Yes. And it slithered up the sidewalk. It slurped up to the gate. It suckered onto the porch. And then, it reached out one long, slimy leg and BAM!"

Kai jumped and laughed again. Delphi was great at telling stories.

"What did the sea monster do next? Did he break down the village?" Kai patted Sammy on his head.

"No," Delphi replied. "Because he got blasted with a Storm Blaster. He cooled off and went back into the ocean."

Kai frowned. "Why?"

"I don't know," Delphi said. "I think he was under a spell."

Kai had thought the same thing too. The octopus monster had seemed confused after he blasted it. But who would put a spell on a sea monster? And why would they want to hurt Pineapple Cove?

The pair turned and walked back to the road that led past Delphi's house. There had been no more sea monster attacks in two whole weeks. It didn't really matter why the monster had attacked. Did it?

"I think—" Delphi cut off. "What was that noise?"

Kai, Delphi, and Sammy stood still and listened.

BANG-slurp-squish-slurp.

Kai and Delphi turned toward each other with wide eyes. Sammy covered his face with his flippers.

CHAPTER 3

RACE AGAINST SLIME

BANG-sloosh-slurpity-squish.

The sound came again! Was that a… monster?

"Come on," Kai said. "I think there's trouble."

Kai and Delphi took off running toward town. Sammy barked and slapped along behind them.

"Almost there!"

Kai wasn't too worried. After all, he had dealt with one of the horrible sea monsters before. He had used the Storm Blaster to chase it off. If there was another one, Kai would run home, get his blaster and get rid of this one too.

Easy.

Kai rushed past Delphi. He held onto his trident necklace, happy that he had it.

The trio burst into the town square and looked around.

All was quiet. The shops' shutters were closed. Doors were shut, too. Normally, the square was full of townsfolk shopping or talking. The tables outside Kai's favorite restaurant, the Salty Clam, were empty too.

"What's going on?" Delphi asked. "Where is everyone?"

Sammy barked and hopped forward on his flippers.

"There!" Kai called.

A monster slurped into view. It looked like a big blob of green jello, except it had two stalks with bobble eyes on the ends. It left a long trail of oozy green slime behind it. The monster was very quick. It slooshed this way and that way, from shop to shop. A long slimy blob arm reached out and grabbed at the door handles or the windows.

Bang! Slam! Scrabbeldy scrape!

The monster left a trail of broken doors and bits of glass. But it didn't take anything.

What does it want? Kai wondered.

Just then, the monster slithered out of the town square.

"Oh no," Delphi cried. "It's going toward the houses. What do we do?"

"Let's follow it, quick!"

Kai and Delphi set off again and chased after the monster. Kai was determined to protect Pineapple Cove. But what was the monster doing here? Captain Hobbs had told them to prepare, just in case, but Kai had been sure no more would come.

"This way!" Delphi called. "I know a shortcut."

The monster had gone straight down the road. It curled through Pineapple Cove and ended in the streets where all the houses were, apart from Aunt Cora's.

Kai and Delphi, with Sammy flippering after them, turned the corner and ran right across the park. They rushed past the rope swing and the rock slide, taking the dirt path that led out of the park.

They sprinted down the road and reached the street. Kai's house was at the end of the block.

The monster blobbed into sight. He trailed slime up the street and stopped in front of the first house.

"What's he doing?" Delphi asked, grabbing Kai's arm.

"It doesn't matter. Let's go!" He pulled free. They had to get the Storm Blaster before the monster did anything else. If Kai could blast him and get him to cool down, then the monster would go away.

The monster *slurpity-slurped* down the street, past the houses. It was surprisingly fast for a slug-looking thing. It stopped only two times, but Kai didn't care. He raced toward his house. To get to it, he would have to go around the monster.

Before Kai could get close, the monster gooped over the front gate of Kai's house. It squirmed up the path and the steps, then burst through the front door. The walls of the house trembled. The windows at the front broke, and glass fell in the garden. A shocked cry rang out inside.

"Hey, what are you doing?" It was a yell that sounded a lot like Kai's mom.

And then the monster came back out. It held

Kai's mom and his little sister, Maya, under each jelly-ooze arm. It slurped down the steps and across the yard. It was out onto the street in two minutes flat.

"Wait!" Kai raced up the street.

But the jelly monster didn't stop. It carried Kai's mom and sister toward the ocean.

CHAPTER 4

MONSTER MISFIRE

"**Q**uick, after them!" Kai called.

The sea monster had already slithered off down the road. If they could just catch him, Kai could get his mom and sister back. He wasn't afraid. Of course, he wasn't.

Kai set off running after the monster. He followed its oozey green slime trail. It glittered beneath the sun.

"Wait." Delphi caught up to him. She grabbed his arm. "Just wait a second, Kai."

"But it's getting away!"

"We need the Storm Blaster first. Otherwise we can't stop it." Delphi's expression was serious. "You get the Storm Blaster from your hiding spot, and I'll go after the monster. That way, it won't escape."

Kai nodded and ran up to his house. The gate was broken. The path was covered in sticky slime. Kai had to jump from one side of the path to the other.

Finally, he reached the front door. He looked back over his shoulder.

Delphi was already at the end of the street. The monster was out of sight.

"Quickly," Kai muttered. "We can't let it get away!" He was inside at last. The house was usually quite warm, but now, a cold wind rushed through it. Furniture was turned upside down, and the floor was covered in broken bits of wood and glass.

Kai took the stairs two at a time. He ran into his bedroom and flung open his closet doors. He had been hiding the Storm Blaster in there, just in case.

Kai had been sure that no more monsters would come to Pineapple Cove. They would be afraid of Captain Hobbs and of Kai, and of the Storm Blaster, of course.

"Hurry, hurry!" Kai threw his clothes over his shoulders. There went a striped shirt, a pair of shorts. A flip-flop. That one landed on the dresser in the corner. Kai pulled out a round sports ball next. Finally, he found the blaster.

He had hidden it here, in the perfect place. No one would expect to find it under a pile of his clothes and shoes!

He lifted it out and tucked it against his side.

Kai left his bedroom messy and ran down the stairs again. He leaped over the green slime and onto the porch, then down the ruined path and out the rickety gate.

He took off down the road after Delphi and the monster. His heart beat *pit-pat-pit-pat* in his chest.

Kai ran around the outside of the island, following the long trail of slime. Some of it was glittery. All of it was wet. It soaked into the sand and made a dangerous goop. He stepped on a little of it by accident, and it sucked on his foot.

He was caught! Kai yelled and tugged his

foot, but it was no use. He was stuck in the goopy sand!

"Delphi!" he yelled. "Sammy!"

A bark sounded in the distance, and Sammy appeared at the end of the road. He flippered over to Kai.

"Help, Sammy. I'm stuck. The monster's getting away!"

Sammy chomped down on the back of Kai's shirt and pulled.

"Again," Kai yelled.

Sammy tugged a second time, and then a third.

Glop-pop!

Kai's foot popped free. "Yuck!" He shook off the goop. "Quick, Sammy, which way did they go?"

Sammy barked and led Kai down the beach. Delphi was there. She stood in the water, up to her ankles, yelling and throwing small stones. "Hey, you, get back here. You get back here, right now!"

The green goop monster had slurped into the shallow water.

"Stop right there," Kai said, and lifted the Storm Blaster. "From the oceans cold and warm, I summon Poseidon's storm!" He pointed it at the monster and let loose a quick blast of coolness. "Take that!"

But the blast of silvery-blue went wide. It missed the monster completely.

The jelly-ish creature disappeared beneath the waves, taking Kai's mom and little sister with it.

"Try again," Delphi shouted.

But it was too late. They were gone.

Kai gripped the Storm Blaster and stared at the waves, the beautiful blue ocean. The monster had left bubbles behind—maybe they could chase it?

Delphi nudged Kai. "Come on, we have to get Captain Hobbs. He'll know what to do."

CHAPTER 5

THE HIDDEN MESSAGE

"This way," Delphi said. "Captain Hobbs is waiting at my aunt Cora's house, remember?"

Together, Delphi, Kai and Sammy tore off across the sand. They had to dodge the slime trail the monster had left behind. Some of the green goop had dried a bit, now. Kai was slower than usual. He was a pretty good runner, but he couldn't stop thinking about what had happened.

He had missed the shot! Why? He was able to blast the giant octopus monster before... Why did he miss the green blob monster today? Maybe he needed the training with Captain Hobbs, after all. But it was too late to worry about that. Kai's mom and sister were gone. Kai wouldn't let the monster get away with it. He would bring his family back.

"Hey, what's that?" Delphi asked.

"What?"

Delphi pointed at a slip of paper stuck in the slime on the sand. "There, see? What do you think it could be?"

Kai and Delphi slowed down. The slime was almost as hard as a rock now.

"It's a note. Hey, and it has your name on it!" Delphi said.

They tried pulling it out, but the goop was too hard. "What do we do?" Kai asked. "We have to get it out of this gross gunk."

A muffled bark sounded behind them.

"Oh, of course!" Delphi shouted. "Sammy, you're a genius."

The sea lion held Kai's big red clam bucket in his mouth. He often left it behind on the beach, tucked behind their favorite rocky spot to sit. Kai and Delphi loved collecting fresh clams in the bucket together.

Now, it was empty.

"We can fill this with water." Delphi suggested. "Maybe if we make the slime wet again, we can get the note out." She hurried to the water and filled the bucket, then brought it back.

Together, they poured the water onto the goo, carefully.

"I'll get the note," Delphi said.

She held onto the end of it as the goo loosened. Finally, she pulled the note free and held it upright. "Got it!"

"Great!" Kai dumped the rest of the water onto the goop, then walked his bucket back to the rocks. He tucked it into his hiding spot. "What does it say?"

Delphi had gone pale. It was strange for her to look pale at all—she was very tan from lots of time in the sun. "Come look at this." She held out the note.

Kai took it from her and read out loud, "Dear Kai. We have taken your mom and sister. You must hand over the Storm Blaster within twenty-four hours or we will keep them forever!" The note wasn't signed, and the bottom part was torn off. But there was a strange blue liquid on it. It had dried on the paper.

Kai's heart was beating fast. "Well, at least we know my family is safe, for now." He looked down at the note again. "But it doesn't say where we're supposed to go!"

"Oh no! What do we do?" Delphi pressed her hands over her mouth.

"Maybe Captain Hobbs can figure this out?" Kai hoped so. Otherwise, they would never be able to find his mom and sister. But they couldn't give up the Storm Blaster either. It was meant for a Protector. "Come on, Delphi. We need to get to Aunt Cora's house, right away."

They hurried into town. Lots of people had already come out of their houses to look at the damage. It wasn't too bad. Some of the roof shingles hung loose or bricks were broken. The florist's shop sign hung sideways and creaked in the wind. The baker's shop had a broken window, and bread loaves spilled out onto the road. The streets were missing a few stones here and there, as well. The air smelled of fresh, salty sea. Still, the people of the town were upset.

A monster attack, again?

Kai and Delphi had to run past all of them in the town square. They didn't answer any questions. They took their favorite shortcut across the park, then onto the road that led along the beach and right up to Aunt Cora's house.

The house looked just as Kai remembered it, complete with a front porch and seashell stepping-stone path. It was rickety and twisty, and three stories high. It reminded Kai of magic. And now, he knew magic *could* be real.

They went inside and found Captain Hobbs sitting at the dining room table, enjoying a refreshing piña pop. He smiled at them as they entered.

"Captain Hobbs, we need your help!" Kai announced. "A monster has attacked the Cove, a big, green, blobby one, and it took my family."

Delphi handed over the note. "Here, look at this, Captain."

Captain Hobbs read it quickly, his bushy eyebrows lifting and falling in time with his reading. "This isn't good."

"What are we going to do? Who do you think left the note?" Kai asked.

"I'm not sure yet. But what's this?" Captain

Hobbs pointed to the blue stain on the paper. "Slime, hmmm. We need to figure out which creature made it. Then we can find out where it came from. I bet your aunt knows more about this."

"That's a great idea," Delphi said. "Aunt Cora knows just about every animal in the sea."

Captain Hobbs rose from his seat. "Come on, Kai. Let's go talk to Cora. We'll get your mom and sister back, don't worry."

CHAPTER 6
I HAVE AN IDEA

Kai, Delphi, and Captain Hobbs left the dining room to find Aunt Cora.

"She said she was going upstairs to do some painting," Captain Hobbs said.

"Oh! I know the way." Delphi led the group up the rickety stairs, past the cages and wonderful tanks full of bubble-blowing fish and tiny seahorses. Kai waved at Finley, and the fish flapped his fin at Kai. Finley smiled his wicked, toothy smile, and Kai grinned back. They reached the second floor of the house and made their way down a long, curving passage.

"This house is huge." Kai peered around once they reached the third floor. He had never been up here before. It seemed impossible that the house could be this big inside.

Sparkly pictures in wooden frames decorated the walls, mostly of painted sea creatures or old, worn maps.

Finally, Delphi knocked on a hardwood door at the end of the passage.

The door opened. Aunt Cora was full of smiles as usual, but soon a big frown turned her lips down at the corners. Kai and Delphi told her all about the green blob monster and how it had taken Kai's mom and sister.

"It was a different monster than last time!" said Delphi.

"We couldn't stop it." Kai bowed his head.

"Oh, you poor dears," Aunt Cora said. "Let's go downstairs and I'll make us some tea. It always helps me see things more clearly." She put her hand on Kai's shoulder. "Together we'll come up with a plan to get your family back."

They followed Aunt Cora back down the twisty stairs and into the kitchen, past the amazing creatures and tanks and cages. The kitchen had charming seashell counters and smelled of coconut.

In no time, they had their tea and coco-nutty cookies and were telling Aunt Cora about the ransom note.

Kai loved Aunt Cora's cookies, but he didn't have much of an appetite. He took the ransom note out and put it on the table. "Look, Aunt Cora, it's got this strange blue ink all over it. Do you know what it is? Or where it comes from?"

"Let me see." Aunt Cora lifted the note and placed it right against her nose. She sniffed the stain, turned the note upside down and the right way around. Her large hazel eyes twinkled and narrowed. "Sirenia Orbis."

"Huh?" Kai saw from Delphi's blank stare that she was as confused as he was.

"It comes from Sirenia Orbis: the Mermaid World," Aunt Cora clarified.

Delphi gasped. "Mermaid World?"

"How do you know?" Kai perked up.

"This gel comes from a special type of blue

jellyfish, also known as the 'dancing jelly.' It lives very far underwater, and it only comes to the surface once a year, right near the entrance to the Mermaid World. The monster must have come from the place where the jellyfish live."

Delphi stared at her aunt with wide eyes. "But how do we get there?"

Captain Hobbs winked at them. "Leave that to me."

Delphi squirmed in her seat. "Oh, this is so exciting. We know where to find Kai's family! *And* we get to explore a whole new world. Oh please, Aunt Cora, can I go? I need to help Kai find his mom and Maya."

Aunt Cora screwed up her lips like she'd tasted a lemon.

"Don't worry," Captain Hobbs said. "I'll be with them every step of the way. I know how to get into Sirenia."

"All right." Aunt Cora took a bite of her crumbly cookie. "But what are you going to do about the Storm Blaster?"

"I have an idea." The Captain scratched his bushy beard. "I have a few merpeople friends. One of them is a master blacksmith and owes me a favor. I bet, if I find him, he'll make a copy of the Storm Blaster for us."

"But Captain Hobbs, how does that help?" Kai asked. "Will we have two blasters to use then?"

"Well, if we have a copy of the Storm Blaster, we can hide the real one, and trade the fake one for your mom and sister. The copied Storm Blaster won't be infused with Poseidon's power, so it won't work. And the true Storm Blaster won't fall into the wrong hands."

Kai liked that idea. This way, he would get his family back *and* keep the Storm Blaster.

Suddenly the dining table started to rumble and shake. Kai jumped backward. "What is that?!"

"Is it an earthquake?"

"Is it a monster?"

Delphi burst out laughing and pointed under the table. Kai leaned down and saw Sammy lying on the floor, snoring.

Everyone relaxed, and Captain Hobbs continued sharing his plan.

"My merman friend probably knows where those jellyfish live too. We could find the kidnappers before they even know we're coming!" Captain Hobbs clapped his big hands together and rubbed them. "Yes, that should work just fine. Are you ready, kids?"

Kai grabbed his trident necklace and held it tight. "I'm ready. Let's go!"

CHAPTER 7
SIRENIA ORBIS

The group boarded Captain Hobbs' ship just before sunset. The waves splashed against the side of the boat as they sailed. The sky was clear, but turning a deep orange. Seagulls cawed overhead.

Aunt Cora refused to join them on their journey, but she wouldn't explain why.

Kai gripped the Storm Blaster and stood near the wheel. A strange wooden lever poked out next to it. Kai reached out to pull it.

"Don't touch that!" warned Captain Hobbs.

"Why? What does it do?" asked Kai.

"Never you mind that now; we're almost there." The captain steered them toward the magical rock archway that was actually a portal. It was the same one they had used to get to Poseidon's Island.

"This is the same place as last time." Delphi patted Sammy's blubbery head.

"Yes, we're going to use the portal to get to the Mermaid World." Captain Hobbs pointed at Kai and Delphi. "You two must go to the front of the ship and say, 'by Poseidon's will, take us to Sirenia Orbis,' and then it will open up for us."

Kai and Delphi hurried to the prow of the boat. They held out their trident necklaces. "By Poseidon's will, take us to Sirenia Orbis."

The gap between the stones of the archway shimmered. There was a bright pink-blue flash. And then, the portal showed a view of the other side. A bright sunny day, and a white sandy beach. On the beach, there was a long dock, and a set of steps that led into the water.

Two merpeople guards floated in the water next to it. They wore their hair in long braids. They flipped their shimmery tails, dove under the water and came back out again.

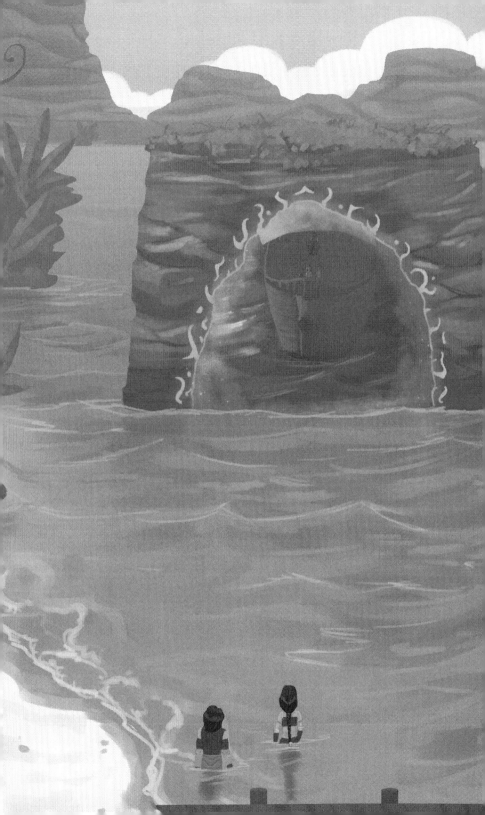

"Here we go!" Captain Hobbs called out. "Everyone hold on to something."

Kai grabbed hold of the railing and tucked the Storm Blaster against his chest.

Quick as could be, the captain sailed them underneath the archway's glimmering rocks and into the sunny waters on the other side.

"It's morning here!" Delphi cried.

"It's the magic of Sirenia," Captain Hobbs replied. "It's always morning here." He steered their ship to the dock. Kai and Delphi dropped the anchor and let down the gangplank.

"Who goes there?" The merman guard lifted himself out of the water. He leaned against the steps.

"Captain Hobbs." The captain gave a salute. "And this is Kai and Delphi."

Sammy barked twice. "And this is Sammy."

Delphi's eyes were round. "Look at their beautiful blue tails," she whispered.

"I'm here to speak with Hermes," the captain continued. "He can vouch for us."

"Hermes?" The guards looked at each other.

The female guard nodded. "Wait right here. We'll find him." And then they disappeared beneath the surf.

"The Mermaid World is down there?" Delphi asked, rising on her tiptoes. She peered into the water. "How are we going to breathe?"

"Don't worry," Captain Hobbs said. "Hermes can help with that."

Kai licked his lips. He was itching to get down there and find out what was really going on.

Luckily, they didn't have to wait very long.

Hermes erupted out of the water and flashed a golden-scaled tail. He had a friendly face and dark skin and eyes. He held three helmets in his strong hands. "Captain Hobbs!" He laughed. "It's wonderful to see you. I never thought we would meet at the entrance to my world."

"It's good to see you too, Hermes. I wish it were under better circumstances," Captain Hobbs said. "Kai here needs help."

"Hobbs, you know I'll do whatever I can to help you. Do you need to come down into Sirenia?" Hermes asked.

"Yes, please," Delphi squeaked. Her cheeks were flushed. She was very excited about meeting a real-life merman.

"Take these." Hermes flipped the helmets at them one at a time, using his sparkly tail. "They will help you breathe underwater."

"Thank you," the three said together.

The helmet was made of a special glass or crystal. It had gills along the side. Kai put it on and took a deep breath. It was lovely, fresh air.

"What about Sammy?" Delphi asked. "He can only hold his breath for twenty minutes. That's not long enough, is it?"

Hermes raised an eyebrow at his friend, and Captain Hobbs shrugged.

"Of course, I will return in a moment." Hermes dove back into the water, and after a few minutes he returned with a fourth helmet. He handed it to Delphi, and she squeezed it onto Sammy's head.

"Is there anything else I can do?" Hermes asked.

"We also need you to take this and make a copy of it," the Captain whispered, pointing to the Storm Blaster. "But it's very important that nobody else know about this. Can you do that, Hermes?"

"Of course, Captain. You saved my family. You can count on me."

Kai came forward and handed the Storm

Blaster to Hermes. It felt very strange to give it away.

"Good," the captain said. "Then we'll follow you down. Are you ready?"

"I am!" Delphi said.

Kai couldn't stand still a moment longer. He dove into the crystal blue water. Bubbles tickled past his ears as he followed Hermes down into the depths.

CHAPTER 8

AN UNEXPECTED VISITOR

The water was warm, and Kai, Delphi and the captain followed Hermes down, lower and lower. It was easy swimming. Currents carried them, so they didn't have to kick their legs much. The deeper they swam, the colder it got – goosebumps prickled on Kai's arms.

Just when Kai thought it couldn't possibly get any colder, a warm current swished over them. Delphi bumped against him. She was looking up toward the surface of the water.

"I didn't think it would be this far down," Delphi said, twisting her hands.

"You can do this, Delphi. You're almost a better swimmer than me now!" Kai squeezed her hand.

Hermes looped back toward them. "We're almost there," he said.

Delphi nodded, and they continued swimming.

Very soon, they found a forest of green kelp, swaying in the aquamarine water. Between the long stalks, blue and pink lights glowed. They were big see-through shells, glimmering on top of sticks.

Delphi gasped and pointed at them, and Kai laughed. At least Delphi was happy. Kai couldn't help worrying about his mom and sister. But Captain Hobbs seemed to know what was going on, and that made him feel a little better.

They made it through the forest of seaweed and followed the lights, lower and lower. Bubbles *blurped* out of the sides of their helmets.

Buildings and beautiful seashell domes

appeared underneath. There seemed to be a lot of merpeople swimming around the opening to a huge arena. It was full of glistening stone steps to sit on, and in the very center, there was a racetrack. It had seaweed too, but it was much shorter.

"What's that?" Delphi asked, her voice filled with wonder.

"That's the seahorse race." Hermes lowered his voice. "You three wait here while I go make a copy of the blaster. I'll be back in no time."

"Thank you, Hermes," Captain Hobbs said.

The merman split off from the group, speeding away into the water. He was an incredible swimmer with that golden tail.

Captain Hobbs led Kai and Delphi down into the stands. They didn't have to pay anything to sit and watch the races. But Kai could hardly sit still. He wanted to run off and find his family, not sit and watch seahorses race around the track.

"Isn't it amazing?" Delphi asked. "Look at them go!"

They were the biggest seahorses Kai had ever seen, much bigger than the tiny ones at Aunt Cora's house. The creatures were pink or blue or purple or green or… so many other colors. They shimmered as they swept through the water, their eyes narrowed. Merpeople riders clung to their reins but didn't sit on saddles.

"Do you like it?" Another mermaid, who had a long, swishy pink tail and glossy pink hair, smiled at Delphi. "We have seahorse races once a week. They're my favorite!"

"You're so lucky!" Delphi exclaimed. "We only have normal, people races in Pineapple Cove."

"I'm Lily. What's your name?" asked the mermaid.

"I'm Delphi, and this is Sammy," Delphi said.

"It's very nice to meet you." Lily scratched under Sammy's chin. The sea lion made a gurgling purr sound, and Delphi giggled.

Kai folded his arms. He shifted on the spot and looked around. Maybe he could swim off and find the special blue jellyfish by himself?

"Are you all right, Kai?" Captain Hobbs asked.

"I want to get going."

"We have to be patient. We can't do anything without the Storm Blaster," the captain whispered. Cheers rose up around them as another seahorse race started.

"Right, the Storm Blaster." Kai slumped down in the stands. The last time he had used it, he had missed! If he had hit the green blob monster with a cooling blast, they wouldn't even be here.

The time passed too slowly for Kai's liking.

The races were lively, but Kai didn't enjoy them as much as Delphi. She and the pink-haired mermaid chatted away, laughing and joking. Delphi looked happier than Kai had ever seen her.

Just then, a squeaky cry rang out, and Blue the Dolphin appeared. He was a flash of blueish-gray. He stopped in front of Captain Hobbs and nudged him.

"What is it, Blue?" the captain asked.

"What?" He untied a kelp scroll from the dolphin's fin and unrolled the message. The captain's jaw dropped. "Mother of Pearl!"

"What's wrong?" Kai asked.

"A very important artifact has been stolen: a crystal egg. It's very powerful. In the wrong hands…" Captain Hobbs trailed off. "It's my duty to protect it. Well, it used to be, anyway."

"Then you should go find it, right?" Kai asked.

"Not until we've found your family and I know you're safe. I won't leave you two alone." The captain looked around at Delphi and her new mermaid friend. "We need to, well, you know... find the jellyfish."

"The jellyfish?" Lily asked.

"Yes, we're looking for a very specific type of glittery blue jellyfish," Delphi replied.

"Oh! I know where they live. They're near a cave west of Sirenia City, just past the Kelp Forest." Lily smiled. "I would take you there myself, but it's time I returned home. I hope to see you again soon." The mermaid winked at Delphi and swished her tail, leaving the stadium behind.

Kai leaped to his feet. "All right, let's go."

"No, Kai," Captain Hobbs said. "Remember, don't be hasty. We have to get the... you know, first." He spoke softly so that none of the other mermaids on the fancy benches would hear. "Hermes should be back any minute—well, speak of the devil!"

Hermes joined them with the blaster in hand. "I ran into a little trouble, but nothing we can't – hey, what's Blue doing here?"

The dolphin chirped happily as Hermes patted him on the head.

Captain Hobbs told him the news of the missing crystal egg. Hermes' mouth fell open. "This is terrible! You must go after it, Hobbs, immediately."

Captain Hobbs shook his head. "I won't leave Kai and Delphi alone. I need to help Kai save his family."

"It's okay, Captain. Hermes can help us. You should go," said Kai.

"Yeah, we'll be safe with Hermes! He probably knows Sirenia Orbis even better than you!" Delphi chimed in.

Worry lines crinkled Captain Hobbs' forehead. "Are you sure you'll be okay without me?"

"Yes!" Delphi and Kai said together.

"I'll take good care of them, Hobbs," said Hermes. "Now go."

"Alright, be safe. I'll be back before you know it." Captain Hobbs took hold of Blue's fin, and the dolphin swam him away.

CHAPTER 9

THE COLLECTOR

"Now, about the Storm Blaster..." said Hermes. The seahorse races had ended, and swarms of mermaids were leaving the stadium. Kai and Delphi looked down at the single blaster in Hermes' hands.

"Why do you only have one blaster?" Kai asked.

Hermes held it out. "This is the copy," he said. "But we have a problem. The Collector took the original."

"Who's the Collector?" Delphi asked, patting Sammy on his head. He gave a concerned *arf*.

Hermes explained it to them quickly. "The Collector is an old squid that collects everything he can get his tentacles on. He's the one who has the copy maker. So, I went to his mansion to copy the Storm Blaster, but right after I made the copy, his guards found me and threw me out. He took the original Storm Blaster!"

"Oh no," Delphi said. "What do we do now?"

Hermes put two fingers between his lips and whistled loudly. Three merpeople appeared, with three seahorses between them. "Here. These seahorses will take us to the Collector's mansion. From there we'll head to the caves west of Sirenia City to find the blue jellyfish."

Delphi squealed and clapped her hands at the sight of the seahorses. She hurried over to one of the creatures.

Kai was relieved—no more waiting around. They were finally on their way to find his family. He looked from the seahorses to the blaster in Hermes' hands. Kai frowned. Once they got the original back and found his family, would he actually be able to save them?

"Don't worry," Hermes said to Kai. "They're well trained."

"I'm not worried. Well, not about the seahorses," Kai said.

Hermes looked at Kai with wise brown eyes. "You know, when I was first learning to be a blacksmith, I was the top of my class. Everything came easy to me. I could make lengths of chain that went on forever before others could finish a few links."

"Really?" Kai knew very little about the merman.

"Yes, really. But soon I became overconfident and bored, so I stopped practicing. One day, I was asked to build a sculpture for the Queen of Sirenia. I tried my best, but could not finish it in time. It was then that I realized something very important."

"What did you realize?" asked Kai.

"Natural talent can only get us so far. Patience and practice are how we accomplish great things." Hermes held out the copied blaster to Kai. "Now, let's go get the Storm Blaster and save your family." Kai took the copy from him and nodded.

Hermes helped them get on the seahorses. Delphi's was pink with yellow stripes, and Kai's was a deep sea green. Hermes' seahorse was the biggest of them all, and a lovely purplish-blue.

Kai slipped and nearly fell off his a few times, but Delphi seemed just fine. She sat

straight and stroked her seahorse's neck. It made a strange purring noise and leaned its head against her hand.

"Hang on tight to the reins. They go very fast," Hermes told them.

"Keep up, Sammy," Delphi said over her shoulder to her sea lion friend.

And then they were off.

The seahorses zipped through the water so fast, Kai's stomach did a loop-de-loop. Delphi shrieked and giggled. Sammy flippered through the water, following closely behind.

They swept over the gorgeous mermaid city below, then through streets with shell walkways. The windows of shell houses had glass that shimmered in a rainbow of colors. It was all so beautiful.

Some of the houses had long, clear chimneys that made bubbles. Each time a bubble popped out, it went *bloop*, and Kai and Delphi would giggle.

"This place is… It feels right," Delphi said.

"What do you mean?" Kai asked. They sped down the street, past mermaids who smiled at them.

"I don't know. It seems like everyone here is friendly. No one has teased me or told me that I'm weird. And Lily was so nice. She told me all about Sirenia City and the seahorse races every week. I wish I could race seahorses."

"It's nice here," Kai agreed. "But I miss Pineapple Cove."

"I don't," Delphi said. "Not that much."

Kai opened his mouth to ask why, but Delphi swung behind him as they passed between two 'blooping' houses. Bubbles bounced off their helmets and popped noiselessly.

The further they went, the quieter it became. The seahorses brought them outside the mermaid city and through a kelp forest with swishing leaves.

Finally, the seahorses slowed. They swept toward a strange-looking wall made out of stone and dirt. Then they swished over it, and Kai gasped. Delphi did too.

A palace lay in front of them, if it could be called that.

It was higgledy piggledy, made out of stones and bits of broken seashells. Some of its rooms seemed to have been glued on crooked, and still others were connected to it by thin bridges of kelp rope.

"Down here." Hermes led them down to one side of the palace. He slid off his purple seahorse, and Kai and Delphi did the same.

"The Collector has the Storm Blaster inside," Hermes told them.

Kai wanted to run inside right away but stopped himself. He remembered what Hermes had told him. "So, what's the plan?" asked Kai.

"You two will have to sneak in," Hermes whispered. "I can't go back because they know what I look like, but they don't know you. They might think you are friends of the Collector, since he has so many strange friends."

"How do we get in?" Delphi asked.

Hermes showed them the open windows near the kelp rope on the side of the palace. "There. You will have to sneak down the hall and find the Blaster. Good luck."

CHAPTER 10
A TRADE OF JEWELS & JUNK

Kai and Delphi swam up to the window together. Kai held the copied Storm Blaster to his chest.

The closer they got, the harder and faster Kai's heart beat. They had been in the Mermaid World for a long time now. Which meant Maya and his mom had been there even longer. What if they didn't have the breathing helmets like Kai and Delphi did?

Kai was itchy all over to run off and find them.

"In here," Delphi whispered.

They entered a lopsided window that didn't have any glass. A long passageway with a dirt floor and shimmery seashell walls lay in front of them. There were doorways that led off into different rooms on either side.

"What now?" Delphi asked. "How are we supposed to find the Collector?"

Kai shrugged and set off. He had to be in here somewhere. They hurried down the hallway, checking each room. A lot of them had piles of gold or silver coins, glowing jewels and crowns, and others had garbage, like shiny chipped seashells or bottles. The Collector seemed to like all of it, and he put the gold jewels and cases next to the bottles and caps.

Delphi and Kai wandered down the hall.

Footsteps stomped toward them, and a pair of guards rounded the far corner.

"Hey!" one of them said. "What are you doing here?" He had tentacles where his mouth should have been, and a big mustache. He pointed his spear. "Intruders."

"No, we're not intruders," Delphi said quickly. "We're here to see the Collector. We have a special gift for him." She pointed to the copied Storm Blaster in Kai's arms.

"Oh. All right. This way." The guards marched them down the hallway and into a grand room.

The Collector floated above a throne made out of glassy seashells. He clutched the real Storm Blaster in his tentacles. "What's this?" he asked. "Another back scratcher?"

Kai and Delphi looked at each other. The

Collector thought the Storm Blaster was a back scratcher?

"Yes," Delphi said. "You have to give us that one because it's actually… um. It's…" She didn't seem to know what else to say.

"That Blas--I mean, back scratcher doesn't work properly," Kai said. "Here, I can show you the difference."

Kai walked up to the Collector. "May I show you?" he asked.

"Yes." The Collector's voice was wet and wobbly, and his beady black eyes focused on Kai.

Kai pumped the handle on the copied Blaster. "See? This back scratcher releases bubbles that feel great on the skin. The one you have doesn't do that. Let me show you." Kai reached for the blaster.

"No!" The Collector gripped the real Storm Blaster to his chest. "This one is mine!"

Delphi bit her lip.

Kai's stomach grew nervous and squirmy.

The guards stood in the doorway and watched them closely.

What now?

"All right," Kai said. "You can see for yourself. Just pump the handle like this and see what happens." Kai motioned with the copied Blaster, and the Collector did the same. He pointed the real Blaster at his squiddy face. "Now, pump the handle here," Kai instructed.

The Collector pumped the handle on the Blaster. Nothing happened. He tried again and still nothing. "Argh, it's broken!" He looked greedily at the blaster in Kai's hands. "Okay, I'll trade you."

Kai and the Collector swapped blasters. As Kai turned and began to walk away, the Collector spoke again. "On second thought, I'll take both. Guards!"

"Blast him, Kai!" Delphi shouted.

Kai spun around and quickly muttered the words: "From the oceans cold and warm, I summon Poseidon's storm." Kai aimed the blaster at the Collector, and a cool blast of white hit him in the face. Immediately, he dropped the copy.

"Got it!" Delphi shouted as she scooped up the blaster.

"Get them!" one of the guards yelled.

Delphi grabbed Kai by the arm and pointed to the window behind the Collector's throne. The big old squid floated around, shaking his head and muttering. He couldn't understand what had happened.

Quickly, Kai and Delphi swam out of the window and past the kelp ropes, down to the waiting Hermes and Sammy.

"We did it!" shouted Delphi. "Kai blasted the Collector! We have both the original and copy."

"Well done," Hermes said. "You'd better get out of here, now. I'll keep the guards busy and join you in a moment."

"Which way is the cave west of Sirenia City?" Kai asked as they mounted their seahorses again.

"It's that way," Hermes said, and pointed.

A yell sounded from the front of the palace, and five guards ran out. They held ropes and chains in their hands.

"Go, quickly!" Hermes cried.

Delphi and Kai jumped onto their sea horses and sped away, with Sammy following closely behind.

CHAPTER 11

THE DANCING JELLY

The trip through the kelp forest was very tickly. The seaweed was soft and brushed against Kai's arms and face. He didn't laugh, though. He couldn't stop worrying about Maya and his mom. He did feel better about his ability to use the Storm Blaster now.

Finally, they made it through the forest and stopped in front of the entrance to a cave. It was blocked by a door, which was covered in glittery blue jellyfish.

"I think this is the place," Delphi said, letting go of the reins of the seahorse. It stayed where she left it.

The cave was surrounded by bright yellow seaweed. It swayed from side to side, and blue jellyfish drifted past.

"We'll have to pull the jellyfish off the door," Kai said.

Sammy nudged one of the jellyfish with his nose. It let out a puff of glittery goo, and Sammy whined and shook his nose.

Delphi got a closer look at the door. "No, Kai, I think they're stuck to it. And we can't touch the jellyfish without getting stung." She sighed inside her waterproof helmet. "I don't think we will be able to get inside without getting them free."

Kai chewed on the inside of his cheek. But how could they do that? He stared at the graceful creatures, moving to their own rhythm.

"Oh, I have an idea!" Delphi exclaimed. "We should sing them a song!"

"Huh?" Kai was totally confused.

"Remember what Aunt Cora said? About how this type of jellyfish is known as the dancing jelly?" Delphi asked.

It finally hit Kai. "Oh, yeah!" He closed his eyes and thought for a moment. "I know a song... My mom taught it to Maya and me."

Delphi nodded. "Let's try it."

Kai started out softly and then sang louder as the words came back to him.

Oh the sea, the ocean, the ocean, the sea
It all means the very same thing to me
The sea, the ocean, the ocean, the sea
I live on land but the sea is for me

When I was a babe, my dad said to me
The ocean's a treasure, rare as can be
Just hear me, my dear, oh, listen to me
The greatest treasure, beautiful sea

♦

"It's working!" Delphi whispered. "Keep singing, Kai."

Sure enough, the jellyfish began floating away from the door, swishing their bodies back and forth. Delphi joined Kai in the singing, and even more jellyfish started dancing. Kai never knew she had such a nice singing voice. Sammy joined in too, with an *arf* here and an *arf* there.

When I was five, my dad said to me
The call of the deep is a mystery
You cannot resist the stormy plea
The deep blue magic, beautiful sea

When I was ten, my dad said to me
The creatures so deep are family
I wish I had gills so I could swim free
With creatures so deep, beautiful sea

And now I'm all grown, with little ones wee,
I tell them their mother is the sea
She gives food and water, all that is key
Mother to us all, beautiful sea

Soon the last of the jellyfish had detached from the door. They swirled from side to side, up and down. Kai stopped singing and grinned. They'd done it. He handed the Storm Blaster to Delphi to hold, and she hid it under her shirt.

Kai had the copy, and Delphi had the real Blaster. The kidnapper wouldn't expect them to have two, and he wouldn't expect Delphi to blast them. Kai was nervous, but ready. Nothing would stop him from getting his family back!

They moved toward the opening. But, oh no! It wasn't open at all.

It was still blocked by a stone door, covered in strange squiggly markings.

"How do we open the door?" Kai asked.

"That's easy," Delphi said. "It's a riddle."

"Wait, you can read that?" Kai asked. "But

it looks like… a different language."

"Yes, I can read it. Hold on a minute." Delphi squinted at the squiggly writing. "It says, 'What is hard but soft, glitters like a gem in the sun, and is priceless to its owner but has no value?'"

Kai blinked. He had no idea. He wasn't very good at puzzles. "Um? A Jellyfish?"

The door didn't budge.

"A star?" He guessed again.

Still, the door didn't open. What would they do now? What if they couldn't get inside?

Kai looked over at Delphi. She was staring at a school of fish that were swimming past, moving this way and that. Sammy looked at the fish too and licked his lips.

"I've got it," Delphi said, and raised her finger. "It's scales. Fish scales."

The door gave a terrific rumble. It swung open and showed the long, dark passage beyond.

CHAPTER 12

QUEEN OF SIRENIA

The corridor was dark, and a little bit frightening. Colorful lights glowed farther down the hallway, pink and blue like they had seen in the Kelp Forest.

Kai took a deep breath and stepped into the hall, holding his fake Blaster. It wouldn't work, but it was nice to carry it and pretend.

The door slammed shut behind them, and Delphi let out a cry. "It's closing! What do we do?"

Just then, two monsters slurped into view. One was the green blob monster who had taken Kai's family! The other was purple, with one giant eye in the center of its head.

"Hey, where's my family?" Kai asked, pointing the Blaster.

The monsters grabbed hold of Kai, Delphi, and Sammy and brought them down the corridor. Kai didn't struggle. Still, it was scary. They would finally meet the horrible monster who had written the note.

What would he look like? Ugly and brown and...

They were brought into a wide chamber. On the edges, yellow seaweed swished and glowed in the water. Monsters stood between the kelp fronds. There were many different colors, shapes and sizes of monsters, and between them all floated mermaids!

"There you are." A beautiful mermaid with long, pink hair and a matching tail sat on top of a throne at the end of the room. "It took you long enough to find me."

Kai was shocked. It was Lily from the seahorse races.

"No!" Delphi said. "Lily? What on earth are you doing here?"

"My name isn't Lily, you silly girl. I'm Amphi, Queen of Sirenia Orbis. I knew you had the Storm Blaster all along, because my fish have been watching you from shore."

Amphi swam off the throne. "And I'm the one who took your family. Bob! Bring them out."

The green gloopy monster slurped into view. Bob held Kai's mom and sister under either arm. They had on helmets to help them breathe too. They didn't seem hurt, but Maya's eyes darted around like she was looking for an escape.

"Give me my family back," Kai demanded. He was relieved that they were safe. Now was the time to act. He raised the fake Blaster and aimed it. "If you don't, I'll have to give you a blast." It was all part of the act. Amphi had no idea that his blaster didn't work.

"Not so fast," Amphi replied with a swish of her tail. "If you blast me, you will never get your family back. You must hand over the Storm Blaster, now. Give it to me."

"Why are you doing this?" Delphi asked. "Why do you want the Storm Blaster? It's not meant for you. It's for Poseidon's Protectors."

"You know why. You and Kai have been talking to Poseidon. You are his favorites!"

Amphi pouted. "He never visits me anymore. Once I have the Storm Blaster, he will finally come see me to retrieve it." Amphi pointed at Kai, then waved to his mom and sister. "Hand it over, or you will never see your family again."

Kai's heart skipped a few beats. It was time for them to put their master plan into action. The only problem was, they hadn't expected to use the Blaster on a mermaid. Would it cool her down the same way it had cooled down the octopus monster?

He looked over at Delphi, who nodded.

"That's right." Amphi swished forward, waving her tail from side to side. She put out a hand. "Come. Give the Blaster to me." She paused. "Bob, bring the prisoners forward."

All around the inside of the lair, the monsters and mermaids watched. Some of them had come a little closer. They probably thought he would fire the Blaster.

Kai took one step forward and then another. He lifted the copied Storm Blaster and held it out.

CHAPTER 13
A SECRET REVEALED

Kai's mom and sister hurried forward. Finally, they were next to Kai, and then behind him and safe with Delphi. Sammy flopped in front of them, puffed out his chest, and barked loudly.

"Here," Kai said, holding up the fake blaster. "Take it."

"A-ha!" Amphi cried, grabbing the copied Storm Blaster. She pointed it at them. "Now, you're going to tell me where—"

"Now, Delphi!" Kai yelled.

Quickly, Delphi drew the real Storm Blaster out from under her shirt. She lifted it and pumped the handle. Nothing happened. She tried again, and still nothing happened.

Delphi looked over at Kai with wide eyes. "Why isn't it working?"

Then Kai remembered. "The words! You have to say the words!"

"Oh, right!" Delphi said. "From the oceans cold and warm, I summon Poseidon's storm!" The blaster glowed, and a long blast of cool blue-white shot out of its end. It struck Amphi right in the chest.

Amphi closed her eyes and shook her head. Her expression went from an angry frown to calm and peaceful.

Delphi blasted the other mermaids and monsters who came forward, and each time, the anger washed away. They were, finally, all calm.

"Oh my," Amphi said, and dropped the fake Blaster. She pressed her hand against her forehead. "Oh my goodness."

"Please, let my friends and family leave," Kai said.

Amphi nodded. "Of course, of course. I'm so sorry. I wasn't thinking straight. I was just so upset because I haven't heard from Poseidon in quite a while. I thought he was ignoring me. I thought if I had the Storm Blaster, I could get him to pay attention to me again. That's what a friend told me, anyway…"

"We haven't heard from him either," Delphi said, helpfully.

Kai's mom and sister rushed over to him. Kai's mom gave him a big hug and a mushy kiss on the cheek. "Are you all right?" she asked.

"I'm fine, Mom." The danger was gone now. "Are you two okay?"

"I was afraid," Maya said. "Kai, I tried to protect Mom, but the monster was too big."

"It's okay, Maya, you did a good job. You're both safe now." Kai hugged his little sister and his mom again. It was difficult to let go of them. He had missed them and worried so much.

All around the room, the monsters and mermaids were relaxing. They were talking, now, or dancing to soft music that one of the monsters made using two strings of kelp. Everyone was happy again. It was hard to believe that just moments ago, it had been so tense.

Amphi swam closer, and Delphi came up beside Kai. Delphi gave him the Storm Blaster. He tucked it into his waistband.

"I really am so sorry. But, you haven't seen Poseidon? Truly?"

"No, we haven't seen him."

"That's strange. He's been quiet. Too quiet," Amphi said, pressing her finger to her chin. "But never mind that now. I want to apologize to you. You are all free to go… unless…"

"What?" Delphi asked.

"Would you like to attend a banquet with us? We were going to hold one for Poseidon tonight, but I don't think he will come. It will be my way of apologizing to all of you. Especially to you," Amphi said, nodding to Delphi.

"Why me?" Delphi asked.

"Because you are part mermaid."

Kai and Delphi gasped. Was it true?

Delphi *had* washed up on the beach of Pineapple Cove many years ago. She understood the mer language on the door. She was also a surprisingly good swimmer...

"I can't believe it," Delphi said. "Amphi, Lily, I mean… you lied to us once already."

"I'm telling the truth. You were lost at sea when you were very little, but found by a woman who raised you as her own. The woman's name is Cora," Amphi said.

Delphi nodded. "Wow. I'm really part mermaid?"

Kai's stomach sank. What would this mean for Delphi? She seemed to fit in so well in the Mermaid World. What if she decided to stay?

"Yes. So, will you come to our banquet?" Amphi asked. "Before you go on your way to Pineapple Cove?"

Kai and Delphi looked over at Kai's mom, and she nodded. "All right," they said. "We'll come." Kai's little sister Maya seemed happy about it too. She kept staring around at all the mermaids and monsters, blinking like she still couldn't believe what was happening.

"Oh, but only if you make a promise," Kai said.

"What's that?" Amphi asked.

"Don't send another monster to Pineapple Cove!" Kai announced.

Amphi laughed. "I promise I never will. On my honor. The monsters are my guardians. They do what I ask them to out of love. But I was wrong, and they won't ever harm you again. They are actually very sweet creatures when you get to know them. Isn't that right, Bob?"

Bob blinked his bobble eyes at her, and his jelly lips parted into a toothless smile.

"To the banquet we go," cried Amphi.

CHAPTER 14

SALT SHAKES & PROMISES

The banquet was incredible.

There were all kinds of delicious foods. Sweet candied kelp bursts, and pop-bubble fruits, and delicious crispy seaweed fries. The drinks were even better—underwater salt shakes and upside-down sea-cherry fizzers.

Kai could hardly speak. He was too busy eating. Sammy sat nearby and looked like he was in heaven. He chomped away at his fishy treats, only stopping to nuzzle Delphi.

Delphi was seated next to a young mermaid girl with blue hair. They were happy and chatting non-stop. Delphi fit in here, but Kai secretly hoped she wouldn't stay behind. Aunt Cora would miss her, and he would too.

Heads turned toward the doorway as someone new entered the banquet room.

"Hermes! You made it!" Kai and Delphi ran over and gave him a hug.

"I see you managed just fine without me." Hermes raised an eyebrow at them.

"Long story; we'll tell you about it later," Kai said. Hermes nodded and bowed to Amphi before taking his seat at the table.

Amphi lifted her glass of sea-cherry fizzer. "Attention, everyone. It's time for me to make my announcement."

Everyone around the table, including Bob the sea monster, turned to face Amphi. Apparently, poor Bob was quite clumsy. He had already broken three glasses and twelve plates, and the first chair he'd sat on. That was the real reason he had damaged the shops in Pineapple Cove. He had also ripped the ransom note by accident and forgotten to leave it at Kai's house.

"I want to apologize again to the people of Pineapple Cove. I promise I will never send a monster to your town again. This is the first

and last time. I swear to everyone here, all the mermaids and humans. I will never ever cause trouble for Pineapple Cove again. In fact, if you are ever in need, you can count on our help."

Everyone gave a great cheer as Amphi took her seat. She drank down her sea-cherry fizzer and burped. The merpeople laughed. Even Bob the monster jiggled back and forth in his chair.

Kai frowned. "Wait a second." He raised his hand, politely. "Queen Amphi," he said. "What do you mean the first and the last? This is the second monster that's been to Pineapple Cove."

"Oh my," Amphi said. "I have never sent any monster except for poor old Bob."

Bob the jelly monster waved his goopy arm.

"Only one monster," Kai said. "Then who sent the first one? The giant octopus monster that looked like it was under a spell."

None of them had any idea. It was a question for another day. Today was a day to celebrate.

"Oh yes," Delphi said to the blue-haired mermaid. "I would love to visit some time. In fact, I would love to stay for a while."

Kai's stomach turned over. What if Delphi did decide to stay after all? He wouldn't like that one bit.

The rest of the banquet was spent eating, talking, and laughing. Kai had a merry time joking around with Bob the jelly blob. Kai's mom and little sister listened to the interesting stories that Amphi had to tell. Hermes showed off the chain he broke during his fight with the Collector's guards. He was very proud of it.

"This was wonderful," Kai's mom said. "But I think it's time we go home now."

"Yes, thank you for the banquet, Amphi," Kai said.

"It's the least I could do. I behaved terribly."

Amphi chewed on her bottom lip and twirled a strand of pink around her finger. "And if you do see Poseidon, please tell me. I would like to know where he's been."

"We will," Kai said.

The humans rose around the table, all except for Delphi. She hadn't moved, and her eyes were wide.

"Delphi?" Kai asked. "Are you coming?"

Delphi pressed her lips together. "I was thinking… maybe I should stay. It feels like I belong here. And it's not like Pineapple Cove will miss me."

Kai lowered his gaze. His throat got all tight. "If that's what you want, Delphi, then you should do it. But you belong in Pineapple Cove too. You have Aunt Cora and Captain Hobbs and me."

Sammy barked loudly next to Kai. "And Sammy, of course." Kai looked Delphi in the eye. "If you do come back to Pineapple Cove, I promise I'll focus more on training."

"I promise to show you all my inventions!" shouted Maya.

"And I promise that you will always have a place at our table," said Kai's mom.

"Aarf, aarf!" promised Sammy.

Delphi's eyes glistened. "Thank you...for showing me that Pineapple Cove really is my home." Delphi turned to face Amphi. "I can come back to visit, right?"

"Of course. You can come visit us anytime you want," Amphi said. "Hermes, please take them back through the portal to their home."

"Yes, my Queen," Hermes said, bowing again.

Delphi finally smiled and got up from the table. "Okay, let's go home," she said.

Kai, his mom and sister, Delphi, and Sammy followed Hermes out of the banquet hall. They paired up and rode their sea horses back through Sirenia City. Kai was full of smiles now, and he laughed as his green seahorse did somersaults through the water. The ocean was warm as ever, and when they reached the dock above, it was still daytime. A small sailboat waited for them.

The guards waved goodbye to the group as they sailed back through the magic arch. In a flash, the portal closed, and they continued on toward Pineapple Cove.

Kai and Delphi helped Maya and Kai's mom back toward the shore. They stood on the beach, waving to Hermes, the fading sunlight warm on their faces. Strangely, sunset had only just come.

"I'm so glad to be back," Kai's mom said. "It was very interesting down there, but frightening too."

"I'm tired, Mommy." Maya gave a big yawn. "Can we go home now?"

Kai's mom took Maya's hand, and together, the five of them walked home. Once again, Pineapple Cove was safe.

CHAPTER 15
THE CAPTAIN RETURNS

The next day, Kai and Delphi walked along the sandy beach, talking about all that had happened. Sammy flippered along close behind.

"…and the seahorses were amazing!" Delphi said, doing a little twirl in the sand.

"Yeah! And remember the Collector's palace? And the dancing jellyfish?" Kai replied excitedly.

"Of course!" said Delphi. "We got to explore and face real monsters, just like you wanted."

Kai grinned. "Yeah it was a blast. But I think I'm ready to get back to training now." He frowned, thinking about their missing trainer.

Delphi nodded. "Where do you think Captain Hobbs went? Do you think he's okay?"

Kai shook his head. "I don't know. He said he would be right ba--"

"Aarf! Aarf! Aarf!" Sammy interrupted. He was staring out at the ocean.

"Look!" Delphi pointed at the familiar ship coming towards them.

"It's him! It's Captain Hobbs!" Kai shouted. They ran down to the water and waited for the ship to dock.

Captain Hobbs stood in front of the ship's wheel and waved at them. "Kai, Delphi, you've got to come back with me!" he shouted down to them.

"Where? Why?" Delphi asked.

"It's the crystal egg. I need your help to get it back," the Captain said. "Quick, climb aboard and I'll explain on the way."

Kai and Delphi looked at each other and shrugged. They climbed up the gangplank and onto the ship.

"Where do we start the search?" Kai asked. The ship was still facing Pineapple Cove. "And don't we need to turn the ship toward open waters?"

The Captain smiled with a twinkle in his eye. "Water? Where we're going, we don't need water." Hobbs pulled the wooden lever next to the wheel, and the ship started to shake. The sails above began to expand and inflate. Soon the sky above was blocked out by a giant balloon, decorated in purple and green stripes.

"Whoaaaa!" Kai and Delphi shouted. "This is so cool!"

Sammy covered his eyes with a seal flipper.

The ship rose out of the water and into the sky. It was time for their next adventure.

TO BE CONTINUED.

HIDDEN PINEAPPLE ANSWER KEY

There are 13 pineapples hidden throughout the illustrations in this story. Did you spot them all?

CHAPTER 1 = 🍍
CHAPTER 2 = NONE
CHAPTER 3 = 🍍
CHAPTER 4 = NONE
CHAPTER 5 = 🍍
CHAPTER 6 = 🍍
CHAPTER 7 = 🍍
CHAPTER 8 = 🍍
CHAPTER 9 = 🍍 🍍
CHAPTER 10 = 🍍
CHAPTER 11 = 🍍
CHAPTER 12 = 🍍
CHAPTER 13 = NONE
CHAPTER 14 = 🍍
CHAPTER 15 = 🍍

QUESTIONS FOR DISCUSSION

1. What did you enjoy about this book?
2. What are some of the major themes of this story?
3. How are Kai and Delphi similar? How are they different? How did they help each other in the story?
4. What doubts or fears did the characters express in the book? When have you been afraid? How have you dealt with your fears?
5. The Legend of Pineapple Cove Book #2 ends with some loose ends. What do you think will happen in the next book in the series?

For more Discussion Questions, visit
thelegendofpineapplecove.com/bundle

AUNT CORA'S COCO-NUTTY COOKIES

| YIELD: 16 SMALL COOKIES | PREP TIME: 15 MINS |
| COOK TIME: 7 MINS | TOTAL TIME: 25 MINS |

Soft and chewy coconut flour cookies with peanut butter and chocolate, these are a classic Pineapple Cove treat. Make them just like Aunt Cora does for Kai and Delphi!

INGREDIENTS
- 1/2 cup peanut butter
- 2 tablespoons coconut oil
- 1/2 cup brown sugar
- 2 large eggs
- 1 1/2 teaspoons pure vanilla extract
- 1/2 teaspoon baking soda
- 1/4 teaspoon ground cinnamon
- 1/4 teaspoon salt
- 1/2 cup coconut flour
- 1/2 cup chocolate chips

INSTRUCTIONS

1. Preheat the oven to 350 degrees F. Line a cookie sheet with parchment paper or a silicone baking mat.

2. Place the peanut butter, coconut oil, and coconut sugar in a large bowl. Blend together until smooth.

Add the eggs and vanilla and blend again until evenly combined.

3. Sprinkle the baking soda, cinnamon, and salt over the top. Sprinkle in the coconut flour. Blend again until the mixture forms a smooth dough, stopping to scrape the sides of the bowl as needed. Using a spoon or spatula, gently fold in the chocolate chips.

4. With a medium-sized spoon, portion the dough by heaping tablespoons onto the prepared cookie sheet. With your fingers, lightly flatten the dough, as it will not spread during baking.

5. Bake for 7 minutes or until the cookies turn barely golden brown at the edges and feel lightly dry. They will be very soft. Let cool on the baking sheet for 3 minutes, and then transfer the cookies to a wire rack to finish cooling. Repeat with any remaining dough.

6. Enjoy and share with family or friends!

For more recipes, visit
thelegendofpineapplecove.com/bundle

ADD YOUR OWN COLOR TO THE MERMAID WORLD!

BRING THIS UNDERWATER SCENE TO LIFE!

For more coloring pages, visit
thelegendofpineapplecove.com/bundle

THE LEGEND OF PINEAPPLE COVE

KING OF THE SEA

By **MARINA J. BOWMAN**

Illustrated by **Nathan Monção**

CONTENTS

1. Flying Ship . 197
2. The Crystal Egg . 202
3. Lockdown . 210
4. Turtle Mountain . 219
5. Weird Purple Bird . 227
6. Gum Tree . 238
7. Gone Fishing . 244
8. Chasing Waterfalls . 258
9. Rainbow Tunnels . 264
10. Old Friends . 274
11. Secrets . 281
12. Crystals of the Sea . 290
13. Under a Spell . 302
14. Whirlpool . 310
15. Next Mission . 319

EXTRAS

 Pineapple Answer Key . 326

 More LoPC . 327

CHAPTER 1
FLYING SHIP

The wooden ship zipped into the sky. Being a fisherman's son, Kai had been on many boats before—but definitely none that could fly. He leaned over the side to see the puffy clouds above getting closer. The sun warmed his skin.

"Kai! Come see this!" called Delphi from the stern of the ship. She waved Kai over excitedly. Her long hair whirled in the warm wind like a purple-and-black tornado.

Crick-Crack-Creak. The ship's old floorboards squealed under Kai's feet as he walked to the back.

Delphi pointed below. "Look, you can see the whole island from up here!"

Kai leaned over the edge of the ship and gasped. He had lived in Pineapple Cove all his life, but he had never seen it from above before. Poking out of the bright, blue water was a pineapple-shaped island with golden beaches. Kai's eyes trailed along the beach until they found the twisty house on the shore.

"Delphi, your place looks like a dollhouse from up here," Kai laughed.

"You mean Aunt Cora's house," Delphi corrected.

Kai was too distracted by the town square to argue. From so high up, it looked like he could pick up the water fountain and take a sip. Then there were the townsfolk weaving in and out of the shops. They looked just like the ants Kai had watched so many times on the beach while collecting clams.

"Pineapple Cove sure is pretty," Delphi said with a sigh.

Kai nodded. He clenched the gold trident pendant that hung around his neck. He knew being one of Poseidon's Protectors meant going on adventures away from home sometimes. But never in a million years did he think that meant going on a mystery mission on a flying ship.

"Where do you think we're going?" Kai asked Delphi.

Delphi shrugged and giggled. "Up!"

"Well, I know that!" Kai said with a laugh. "But where to?" He thought about how Hobbs had picked them up in the ship for an urgent mission. But all they knew so far was that Hobbs needed help getting the crystal egg back—whatever that was. Kai glanced up at the clouds, but all he could see from this end of the ship was the inflated sail. It looked like a giant green-and-purple-striped balloon.

Delphi sniffed the air and wrinkled her nose. "Do you smell that?"

Kai took a deep breath. He expected fresh sky air, but instead, he inhaled a super stinky smell. It smelled like rotten, cheesy socks.

WHAP! Something slimy and wet landed on Kai's toes. He looked down to see a one-eyed fish with two tails lying on his foot. It was covered in shiny red scales. Except for the glimmering, gold turtle shape on its belly.

Sammy, the sea lion, stood beside the fish. He bounced his blubbery head around excitedly.

"Aarf! Aarf!" Sammy barked.

Delphi laughed. "He found you a gift."

"Why does it look so weird?" Kai asked. But before he could examine it more closely, everything faded to white. The ship rose higher into the sky, and a chilly fog surrounded the boat. Kai rubbed his arms and shivered.

Sammy let out a small whimper.

"It's okay, Sammy. I think we're just going through clouds," Delphi reassured him.

Just as fast as the clouds had rolled in, they disappeared. Kai could once again see Delphi, Sammy, and the strange stinky fish by his foot.

"Sammy!" yelled a gruff voice.

CHAPTER 2

THE CRYSTAL EGG

Crick-Crack-Creak squealed the ship's wood floorboards.

"Sammy!" called Captain Hobbs again, this time much closer. "Where is that little hornswoggler?"

Sammy quickly flippered behind Delphi, his tail still clearly visible.

Captain Hobbs groaned and tilted his head back. "Gee, I wonder where Sammy could be," he said in a softer voice. "Good thing he didn't leave the fish he stole in plain sight."

A little gray flipper poked out from behind Delphi's legs. The flipper slowly dragged the stinky, slimy fish across the floorboards.

Captain Hobbs rolled his eyes. Then he snatched up the fish before Sammy could finish dragging it.

Sammy slowly poked his head out from behind Delphi.

"You can't just go stealing fish," Captain Hobbs scolded. "Especially not this one. We need this fish for Turtle Mountain."

"Turtle Mountain?" Delphi and Kai asked at the same time.

"Turtle Mountain," Captain Hobbs confirmed. "The hiding spot of the crystal egg. And the last place it was seen before it was stolen. While we were on our last mission saving Kai's mom and sister, I received a kelp scroll."

Just the memory made Kai's heart race. That green blob kidnapping his mom and sister had been one of the scariest moments of his life.

"That scroll was sent to me by the Turtle People," Hobbs continued. "They said the crystal egg was stolen, but by the time I got to Turtle Mountain… well, the place was already in lockdown. So I couldn't get in. Only Poseidon's Protectors can, which is why I need your help."

Kai's stomach did a cartwheel. He didn't know what the crystal egg was, but he was excited to hear he was needed. He hadn't met Poseidon yet and wondered if he was really cut out to be a Protector. Kai was glad he had saved Blue the dolphin from the fishing net. He'd made a new friend and gotten his trident necklace for his bravery. But wouldn't a real Protector be chosen by Poseidon himself?

"What's the crystal egg?" Delphi asked. Her question brought Kai's focus back to the mission.

Captain Hobbs took off his hat. He ran his hand through his dark hair, which was peppered with gray strands.

"Long ago, two magic objects were created and infused with the power of the sea and sky,"

Hobbs explained carefully. "A trident for The King of the Sea and a thunderbolt for The King of the Sky. It was a great idea, as enemies didn't dare to go up against the powerful objects. But it wasn't long until the thunderbolt started to malfunction."

"Malfunction?" Delphi said.

"Malfunction," Hobbs repeated. "It wasn't strong enough to hold the power of light, and the light was slowly leaking out. It leaked out so much that the sun faded away. Soon after, the sky became black. Without the power of light, there is no sun."

Delphi gulped. "That sounds bad."

"Very bad," Hobbs said.

Kai agreed that would be a bummer. After all, he really liked sunny days, but he was confused.

"Is no sun really that bad?" Kai asked. "Couldn't they just use lightbulbs for light?"

Hobbs shook his head. "It's not that simple. Without the sun, our food and plants wouldn't grow. In fact, the whole island would freeze. Without the sun, it would be too cold to live for the animals, fish, and townsfolk. Without the sun, Pineapple Cove would be doomed."

Kai's heart pitter-pattered in his chest.

"Okay, so that is very bad," he agreed. "But what does this have to do with the crystal egg?"

"It was the solution. The power of light was originally found in a crystal egg by an explorer in Sky City," Hobbs explained. "And it turns out it was in there for good reason. They learned later that the crystal egg is the only thing strong enough to contain the powerful element. That's why the thunderbolt couldn't hold it like it could the power of wind, rain, and electricity. In fact, the thunderbolt worked great once all the light leaked out."

"What happened to the light that leaked out?" Delphi asked.

"Luckily, with some magic and another crystal egg, the Protectors were able to recapture the power of light," Hobbs answered. "The sun returned, and Pineapple Cove was saved. But now the egg has been stolen and, if the light escapes, I don't think we will ever get it back."

Hobbs pulled a bag of small crystals out of his pocket and began to play with them nervously. The bag had "Hobbs" stitched into it with red thread.

"Legend says that only three crystal eggs exist," Hobbs continued. "There was the first one they cracked on purpose to get the light into the trident. The second egg that the light was recaptured in and later broke by accident. And the third one was stolen from Turtle Mountain. The problem is the Turtle Mountain egg has a small crack. The Turtle People found a way to seal it in a special box, but the light instantly begins to escape when removed. And if the light escapes this egg, there is no other egg for it. We fear the whole island will be plunged into darkness forever."

Kai clenched his fists by his side. He loved his home. And the thought of someone wanting to hurt it made him mad.

"Who would want to do that to Pineapple Cove?" Kai asked. "Did they know the light would escape when they stole the egg?"

Hobbs shrugged. "I'm not sure. I don't know how someone stole the crystal egg, either. Turtle Mountain is one of the safest places in Pineapple Cove. Another Protector named Jasper and I brought the egg there many years ago ourselves… when I wasn't a disgrace and was still a Protector."

Kai and Delphi had been training to be Poseidon's Protectors with Hobbs for a while now. Yet, his past was still a mystery. Kai wanted to know more about why he was no longer a Protector.

BANG!

But now was not the time.

The whole ship shook, and Sammy dove behind Delphi with a whimper. Something had hit the side of the ship. Hard.

CHAPTER 3

LOCKDOWN

Kai grabbed the edge of the ship to steady himself.

"What was that!?" Delphi cried.

A crack of lightning whizzed past one of the ship's balloon sails.

Hobbs leaned over the ship's wooden rail. His eyes widened.

"Mother of Pearl!" cried Hobbs.

Kai and Delphi joined him just in time to see another cannonball firing toward them.

BANG!

The ball smacked against the hull of the ship, knocking everyone on their bottoms.

Green, glittery goop splashed onto the deck. Some of it landed on Kai's hand. It felt slimier than the weird fish.

Kai scrambled to his feet. There were two round holes in the hull of the ship. If they had been in water, they would be sunk by now.

"Atlas," Hobbs yelled into the clouds above. "ATLAS!"

"Who are you yelling for?" Kai asked.

"It's the secret password to stop the slime cannons. ATLAS!"

BANG!

"ATLAS!" everyone called at the same time. Even Sammy threw in his own "Aarf Aarf!" But it was no use.

BANG!

Another slime cannonball hit the ship. This time, it busted right through the big, ballooned sail.

Air shot out from the big hole and the sail

deflated—they were going down.

"No, no! We must go up to the mountain," Hobbs cried. "Help me crank this wheel to inflate the other sail!"

Everyone ran toward a large, red wheel in the middle of the ship. They tugged and pulled, but the rusty wheel wouldn't budge. They were dropping fast, and Kai was having trouble gripping the wheel with the hand that got slimed. It was too slippery.

CREAK!

The wheel finally turned a smidge but quickly got stuck again. Brown rust flaked off on Kai's hands. He remembered his bike and how the pedals wouldn't turn when it got rusty. His mom fixed it with a little grease. Too bad they didn't have grease on the ship.

Kai's slimy, slippery hand slid off the wheel. He cried out in frustration. But wait, maybe that was what they needed!

Kai raced to the side of the ship that the cannonballs had smashed. There he found just what he needed—lots of the slimy, green goop stuck to the side. He hoped this worked, because the ship was falling fast.

"Kai, we need your help!" Delphi cried from the stuck wheel. "What are you doing?"

"I have an idea," Kai answered as he scooped up a handful of slime. He ran back to the wheel and smooshed it into the nooks and crannies.

CREAK! CROOOOOAK!

The wheel started moving. Kai's plan had worked!

They turned the wheel as fast as they could, inflating the new balloon sail—a much bigger, red balloon sail.

"If we can get up to Turtle Mountain, I will drop you off," Hobbs said. "I think I can get close enough to the edge before the ship gets zapped by the bubble barrier. Only Protectors and animals can get through the barrier without being shocked. You will need to go in and find a special compass that will lead us to the egg."

They continued to crank the wheel as Hobbs talked. Kai's arms were starting to hurt. But it was worth it. They were beginning to soar upward again.

"The compass will be hidden in an entrance on the side of the mountain," Hobbs continued. "The entrance will be near a purple ho—"

BANG!

A slime cannonball whizzed past the ship, just missing the newly inflated sail.

"Once you have the compass, bring it up to the Turtle People so they can activate it."

BANG!

The ship shot up through a cloud just in time to miss getting blasted once more. A large mountain with green spots appeared beside the ship. Kai let go of the wheel and gave his arms a shake. They felt like jelly from all that hard work.

"There is Turtle Mountain!" Hobbs cried.

Kai could see how it got its name. The mountain looked just like a turtle. It had an oval body that balanced a round head at the peak and two rocky fins poking out from each side. The cannons that had been chipping away at their ship were mounted right on the turtle's head. They looked like two silver eyes.

Around the entire mountain was the bubble barrier that Hobbs was talking about. It looked like a giant soap bubble with sparks of electricity skipping across the surface.

Kai gulped. He sure hoped Hobbs was right about Protectors not getting shocked by the barrier.

The ship continued to sail upward, high above the mountain.

"Aarf!" barked Sammy.

"I think you're right, Sammy," Delphi agreed. "We're going too high."

"We must go up to go down," Hobbs said.

POP! He yanked the cork out of the sails.

Psssheeeeew!

The air slowly leaked out of the giant, red balloon. The ship sank lower in the sky. They floated through a fluffy, purple cloud that looked like cotton candy. Sammy chomped at the cloud a few times, trying to get a taste.

BANG!

As they broke through the cloud, the cannons spotted them again. This time, they didn't miss. A slimy cannonball barrelled right into the side of the ship.

"We've only got one shot at this," Hobbs explained. "The ship won't take another hit. I am going to get the ship close to the middle of the mountain. You are going to jump out on the edge. And don't forget this. You need this fish to get to the compass." Hobbs tossed the stinky fish with two tails to Kai.

"Can't you land us at the top?" Delphi asked.

"No, the cannons are sure to hit us that high up. And the entrance to the compass is on this level. Once you have the compass, take the staircase to the top of the mountain. Give the compass to Cybil or it won't work. Are you ready?" Hobbs asked as Kai tucked the fish into his pocket.

The ship floated closer to the mountain.

Kai wanted to ask why they needed to go to the top of the mountain and who Cybil was. But there was no time. Kai took a deep breath. He was ready. He and Delphi crouched on the edge of the ship.

Hobbs counted them down. "Five, four, three, two, one."

BANG!

CHAPTER 4

TURTLE MOUNTAIN

Another cannon whizzed past the ship just as Kai and Delphi jumped. Their feet hit the rocky edge of Turtle Mountain, and they both let out a sigh of relief. But Delphi's relief didn't last long.

"Where's Sammy?" she cried, looking for her blubbery friend.

Delphi turned around to the sound of whimpering. Sammy was still standing on the edge of the ship.

"Jump!" Hobbs ordered Sammy. "I can't hold the ship here any longer. If you want to go, go now!"

"Come on, Sammy!" Delphi encouraged.

"Jump, Sammy!" Kai shouted, clapping his hands.

Sammy backed away from the edge of the ship.

"Guess he isn't coming," Delphi sniffled.

"We will meet you at Aunt Cora's," Hobbs yelled. "Lightning strikes are counting down to when the egg's power is released. Once the power leaves the egg, it will be too late and the sun will disappear. By my count, we only have six more lighting strikes, so hurry!"

Just as the ship began to descend, Sammy came flippering toward the mountain. Using the slime from the cannons, he slid across the ship's deck on his belly, launching himself off the side. He looked like an acrobat performer soaring across the sky and landed right into Delphi's arms.

Delphi laughed. "Sammy! Good jump!"

The ship flew under a cloud, and the cannons stopped.

Kai, Delphi, Sammy, and the strange, stinky fish were now alone on Turtle Mountain.

The mountain was eerily quiet. A fine mist danced along the ground with heavy moss that squished with each step they took. The squishy moss gushed water that smelled like mint and made Kai's nose tingle. With the wet moss and puddles of water, Kai wondered if it had just rained.

"ACHOO!"

Kai jumped at the sudden, loud sound. He turned around to see Delphi wiping her nose.

"Sorry," Delphi said. "That smell makes me sneezy."

Branches crackled and snapped under their feet as they made their way to a large clearing. A clearing that was just as still and quiet. In the middle, there was a small village sitting under the gray sky spotted with black rain clouds.

The houses were small and simple, with

woven straw roofs and wood planked walls. Many had vines tangled between them, some with clothes hanging off them to dry. A strong breeze rustled the trees behind them.

Kai wished he had the Storm Blaster. He always felt like a real Protector with it. But in their rush to get on the ship, he had forgotten it at Aunt Cora's. It was too bad, because just one blast

from its powerful water stream could cool down even the angriest creature. Kai knew because they had used it to cool down both an octopus and mermaid on other missions. What if there were angry creatures on Turtle Mountain? Or, what if they ran into whoever had stolen the egg?

"We should see who lives here and if they can help us," Delphi said.

Kai nodded. "We don't have a lot of time. Maybe someone can help us find the purple horse and the opening for the compass."

Delphi giggled. "Don't you mean the purple hose?"

Kai shook his head. "No, I think Hobbs said purple horse."

"And where are we going to find a purple horse?" Delphi asked, crossing her arms.

"Hey, it turns out that you're part mermaid," Kai reminded Delphi. "Isn't anything possible?"

Delphi uncrossed her arms. "True. But I still think Hobbs said hose."

A streak of lightning bolted across the sky.

"Only five more lightning strikes," Kai gulped. "Horse or hose, we need to hurry."

They raced farther into the village, but no one seemed to be around.

Kai went up to a small house made from round stones and knocked at the door.

KNOCK. KNOCK.

But no one answered. Next, he went around to the side of the house. A large tree twisted into an S-shape had long, blue fruit hanging off the twisty branches. As Kai got closer to the tree, his foot smooshed one of the fallen fruits. It splattered on the ground and released a stench that smelled like spoiled milk. Kai gagged.

"I don't think anyone is here," Delphi said, walking toward Kai. She stopped and pinched her nose. "You could at least say 'excuse me.'"

"It's not me!" Kai said. "It's this strange fruit." He scraped the fruit off his shoe with a stick from the ground. "But we have bigger problems. No one seems to be around."

"Then I guess we are on our own," Delphi said. "Let's go find that purple hose."

They searched the area in silence, looking for the entrance to the mountain. Kai looked around the bushes and trees. While Delphi and Sammy searched near the houses. It felt like they had been searching for half an hour before one of the bushes nearby began to rustle.

Kai whirled toward the sound, and that was when he saw it. A small, purple horse butt with a swishing tail was sticking out of the bush.

"Told you it was a horse," Kai said to Delphi.

Kai bolted toward the horse. Something else was sticking out of the bush too. It looked like a white, feathered wing. How many animals were hiding in the bush?

"Wait, Kai!" Delphi warned. "I'm not sure that's a horse."

It was too late. Kai scared the winged animal before he even reached it. It shot out of the bush, spread its fluffy wings, and flew into the sky. It perched itself on a cloud just off the edge of the mountain.

"Oh no! Why would you do that?" came an unfamiliar voice.

CHAPTER 5

WEIRD PURPLE BIRD

A small girl with a turtle shell on her back gazed up at the winged creature on the cloud. She had sky-blue eyes and orange hair that looked like a blazing fire. A crown of flowers was braided loosely into her fiery strands.

"I am never going to get Hera down," she complained, tucking her braid behind her ear. She glared at Kai. "Do you normally just run at animals you don't know?"

"Oh, um," Kai mumbled. "No."

"Then why would you scare Hera like that? I've been looking for her all day."

Delphi squinted at the purple creature sitting

on the cloud. "What kind of animal is Hera?"

The turtle girl shifted her feet. "Oh, she's a… bird."

"Then can't she get down by herself?" Kai asked. "She did fly up there."

"No, she usually doesn't fly. She is too young," the girl said. "She only seems to fly when she is spooked, and I can never control where she goes."

"Are you sure she's a bird?" Kai asked. "She definitely has a horse tail. I saw it with my own eyes."

"How would you know? You scared Hera away before you even reached her," the girl snapped.

"Sorry about that," Kai said. "I was just trying to find the entrance to the mountain."

The girl exhaled loudly and looked up at Hera on the cloud once more. "Can you help me get her down, please?"

Kai shook his head. "We can't. We don't have time. We are on a very important mission to save Pineapple Cove. We need to find the entrance to the mountain beside a purple horse… or a purple hose. Do you know who stole the crystal egg?"

The girl looked down at Kai's pendant. "Oh! You two are Poseidon's Protectors!" she exclaimed. "No, no one up here knows what happened to the egg. It's like some sort of magic was used to make us forget. The whole village is scared. They've been sheltering in the base of the mountain since the crystal egg was stolen. Everyone has been waiting for you Protectors to arrive."

A proud smile stretched across Kai's face.

"Why are you out here and not with everyone else?" Delphi asked.

"I was out helping my dad collect some food and wanted to check on Hera at home. But then she escaped." The girl put her hands on her hips. "Hey, isn't it the job of the Protectors to help those in need? Getting Hera down will only take a second. Then I can show you the opening for the mountain." She trailed off for a second. "I would save Hera myself, but I'm a horrible climber."

Kai's face grew hot with embarrassment. The turtle girl was right. It was their job to help her, and he felt foolish for forgetting that. Yes, they needed to get to that compass right away, but she was going to help them find it.

"Okay," Kai said with a smile. "We will help."

"Kai, can I talk to you?" Delphi said. She yanked Kai away from the turtle girl before he could answer.

"Why should we trust her?" Delphi whispered once they were far enough away that the girl couldn't hear. "Remember what happened when we trusted that mermaid in Sirena Orbis?

She lied to us. What if this turtle girl is just trying to trick us?"

Kai had to admit, Delphi had a point. They barely knew this girl. He looked at the girl as she patted Sammy's head.

"Okay, that's true. But she is right," Kai said. "It is our job as Protectors to help. And she did say she would show us the entrance. We tried looking for it ourselves, but we don't even know if we're looking for a purple horse or hose. And we are running out of time."

Delphi let out a long huff. "Fine. You're right. Maybe we can help her and just keep an eye out for anything suspicious."

"Sounds like a plan," Kai agreed. He wondered if Delphi's sudden mistrust came from the fact that Aunt Cora had lied to her. Cora had known all along that Delphi was part mermaid and never told her. Kai shook his head. Now wasn't the time to think of that, though. They had a weird, purple bird to save. They learned the girl's name was Willow after a quick introduction. Then they got to work.

Willow pointed to a fat tree with a limb sticking off the edge of the mountain. "First, someone will need to climb that tree to get to the clouds."

"You're the best climber out of the two of us," Delphi said to Kai. "So I think you should go."

Kai smiled. "Okay!" He was always happy to be right in the action.

"The easiest way to get up there is to leap from cloud to cloud," Willow explained. "But only the ones with a pink tint will hold you. The white ones you will fall through, so you have to be very careful."

Kai surveyed the clouds in the gray sky. Some were white, while others were black and gray. And if he squinted really hard, he could see a few tinted pink. It would be like hopping from rock to rock in a river, but the fall would be a bit more than a splash. He peeked over the edge of the mountain—there was no ground in sight. Just a thin layer of wispy clouds.

Delphi pulled a thick, leafy vine down from a nearby tree. It was the same type of vine that some of the houses used to hang clothes.

"Here, tie this around your waist," Delphi said. "That way, if you fall, we can pull you back up."

Kai tied the rope around his waist and sprang into action. He clawed his way up the tree like a cat. Then he slithered onto the branch on his belly. Next, he sat on the branch and plopped down on the first pink cloud.

Sammy covered his eyes with his flippers.

Kai hopped to the next pink cloud. And the next.

"Slow down," Willow instructed. "Make sure to look before you leap, and don't spook Hera. She is easily frightened."

Kai did as instructed, stopped, and took a deep breath. A gust of wind pushed the cloud he was standing on, and he started to wobble.

"Woah!" he cried. He stuck out his arms to regain his balance.

After jumping across a few more pink clouds, he was almost at Hera.

Hera sat shaking on a small cloud, her wings lightly fluttering. Now that Kai had a closer look, he knew exactly what she was—a Pegasus. She had the body of a horse with wings like a bird. He thought they were just fairy tale creatures, but now he knew Pineapple Cove was full of magic. So this wasn't too much of a surprise.

"Come here, Hera," he whispered to the shaky Pegasus. "I won't hurt you. I'm sorry I ran so fast at you earlier."

Hera stared at Kai sideways with one of her beady eyes. Kai slowly reached out to grab Hera, who was no bigger than a watermelon. He petted her back and scooped her into his arms. She felt like a ball of silk with her soft, purple fur.

"Aarf! Aarf!" Sammy cheered. But he was quickly shushed by Willow and Delphi.

"Aarf," Sammy said much quieter.

"You have to move very slowly and quietly with her," Willow whispered.

Kai softly leaped from cloud to cloud. He took extra care to check that each cloud was pink. He stood on the last cloud before the tree, almost there. And that was when it happened—a big, black bird swooped down.

"CAW! CAW!" the bird cried at the top of its lungs.

Little Hera bucked, slamming her hooves into Kai's chest. She flapped her wings furiously and darted to the mountain. Kai didn't have any wings to save him, though.

He teetered on the edge of the cloud, trying to regain his balance like he did with the wind. But then the black bird swooped down once more. The last swoop pushed Kai too far back, and he fell off the cloud.

"Ah!" screamed Kai as he dropped down into the sky like a rock.

Delphi and Willow grabbed onto the vine. In the panic, it felt light as they reeled Kai in. They reached the end and found out why Kai was so light—there was no Kai. Just a frayed end.

The vine had snapped.

CHAPTER 6
GUM TREE

"**K**ai!" Delphi screamed over the side of the mountain. "Kai!" Tears stung her eyes as she looked for any sign of him.

BOING!

Delphi gasped as she watched Kai bounce up. But then he fell back down.

BOING!

It wasn't long before he was up again, though. He laughed like seconds ago he hadn't just fallen off a cloud.

"He must have found a gum tree!" Willow said. "Thank goodness."

BOING!

Delphi watched as Kai rocketed up and down in the sky. She let out a sigh of relief.

"A gum tree?" Delphi asked.

"We have trees on Turtle Mountain that grow these thick, flat tops," Willow explained. "They're called gum trees. Most kids around here love to climb them because the tops are bouncy like trampolines. They're so much fun! Some even like to bounce on the ones that stick out from the mountain. I've always been too scared for those."

BOING!

With one last bounce, Kai sprang up to the mountainside.

"That was awesome!" he exclaimed. "I could do that all day. There is a tree down there like a giant trampoline."

"It's called a gum tree," Willow repeated.

Kai laughed. "If I plant some chewed gum

in my yard, can I grow one of those?"

Willow giggled. "That's not quite how they work."

Clip-clop-clip-clop.

Hera trotted over to Sammy and gave the sea lion a big sloppy lick on the nose. Sammy stood frozen, unsure what to do.

"Hera!" Willow cried. She scooped up the creature and hugged her tight.

"You know, she looks a lot like a Pegasus," Delphi said. "Aunt Cora used to read me fairy tales with Pegasus all the time when I was little. They were winged creatures that people would ride in the sky." Delphi looked at how Hera fit in Willow's arms and giggled. "Although Hera only looks big enough for a mouse to ride."

"I thought that she looked like a Pegasus too!" Kai agreed.

Willow groaned and lowered her voice to a whisper. "Fine, she is a Pegasus, but keep your voice down. No one around here can know."

"Why not?" Kai asked.

Willow stroked Hera's head. "She doesn't belong here. She belongs up in Sky City. My father studies creatures, and he found her as an egg on one of his trips up there. There was no momma Pegasus anywhere, so he brought her home and hatched her. She was supposed to go back after she hatched, but..." Willow's bright, blue eyes glossed over. "She's my best friend. And I'm afraid that if people find out she is here, they will send her away."

Delphi patted Sammy's head and smiled. She understood Willow's love for the animal.

"Don't worry, your secret is safe with us," Kai assured Willow.

Willow smiled. "Thanks."

Kai looked up at the sky, which seemed to be getting darker.

"Can you show us the entrance to the mountain now?" Kai asked. "We need to get moving."

"Sure," Willow answered. "Do you have a two-tail fish?"

"I do," Kai said. He smiled and patted his pocket. But his smile quickly turned into a frown.

"What do we need the fish for, anyway?" Delphi asked.

"I can't tell you," Willow said. "But you definitely need it."

Kai started pacing the ground, searching for the fish. He turned his pockets inside out, but all that was left were a few shiny scales.

"The fish is gone!" Kai cried.

A cackling sound came from the tree that Kai had climbed to save Hera. The black bird that had swooped down sat with the fish in his mouth. He spat it out, and they watched as the fish flopped down the side of the mountain.

"Nooo!" Kai shouted.

With one more cackling sound, the bird flew away.

Lightning flashed across the sky. Neither Kai nor Delphi said anything, but they knew time was running out. Only four more lightning strikes until the sun was gone and their home was ruined forever.

CHAPTER 7
GONE FISHING

Kai sat on a rock and cradled his head in his hands. *How could this be going so wrong?* he thought.

Delphi patted Kai's shoulder. "It's okay. Maybe we can find another fish."

Kai groaned. "I have been fishing all my life, and I have never seen a one-eyed fish with two tails. I don't think we will find one in time."

"Actually, I know where you can find one," Willow said. Without waiting for anyone to agree, she ran to the forest.

Kai and Delphi followed their new friend into the forest. The minty smell of moss tickled Kai's nose again, but this area had more than just moss. This part of the forest seemed to have more life than all of Turtle Mountain. There were lots of little creatures hopping around the tall grass and scurrying up the tall trees. Some he had seen before, like the slinky squirrels zipping through the hollow logs. But other animals were new, like the little gold lizards with leathery wings leaping around the forest floor.

The lizards' scales glimmered like pieces of pirate's gold, while their bulging eyes looked like glass marbles with green slits. One lizard stopped to look at Kai with its bulging eyes. It quickly flicked out its tongue to snatch a fat fly out of the air.

The soft sound of rushing water got louder as Willow led them to a pond.

Beside a small, trickling waterfall was a man fishing. Just like Willow, he had bright orange hair and a turtle shell on his back. He paid no attention when they walked toward him. He kept staring at the pond through his round glasses, where his fishing line was submerged.

"This is my Dad, Bion," Willow said. "He comes here to fish all the time and has caught lots of those two-tail fish."

The tip of Bion's fishing rod yo-yoed up and down. Kai knew exactly what that meant—a fish was biting on his line. Bion carefully lifted the rod as he watched the end bobble. But soon, it stopped. After a couple of minutes, he pulled in his line. The fish had run away with his bait.

Bion slumped his shoulders. "Oh well, we have enough for now." He stood and walked over to Kai and Delphi. He smiled at the trident pendants dangling from their necks. "Ah, I knew it was only a matter of time before Poseidon's Protectors showed up."

"They need a two-tail fish," Willow explained.

"I didn't catch any of those today," Bion

said. "But you are more than welcome to borrow this."

"Thank you," said Kai as he took the wooden fishing rod from Bion. "What kind of bait do the two-tail fish like?"

"Try the plump, red berries on the bush over there. They always bite on those," Bion answered as he picked up his backpack and a basket full of regular fish and red berries.

Kai went to get a berry for his hook, and the pond started to swirl.

"Shh. Shh," Willow and Bion softly shushed the water. Just as fast as the swirling started, it stopped.

Kai's eyes bulged in shock. He imagined he looked like one of those little lizards. He had never seen anyone calm water before. He didn't even know that was possible. Okay, maybe for someone like Poseidon. But not just anyone.

"How did you do that!?" Delphi asked.

Bion turned toward Delphi. "Sometimes even water gets angry and needs to be soothed. Shushing it softly usually does the trick." He eyed the purple that streaked through Delphi's dark hair. "You're a mermaid, aren't you?" asked Bion. "But not just any mermaid—an Artemis."

"How do you know?" asked Delphi.

Bion smiled. "It's my job to know these things. And Artemis mermaids always have a colored streak in their hair. Plus, many have special powers."

Delphi shook her head. "Well, I have a streak in my hair. But I don't think I have any special powers."

"Hold on," said Bion as he began digging through his backpack.

Kai listened to the conversation as he hooked the berry on his line. He knew that ever since Delphi found out she was a mermaid, she had wanted to learn more. But she couldn't find anything about where she came from. And worst of all, Aunt Cora—the person she trusted most in the world—had known all along and kept it from her. He knew that if his parents had lied to him all his life, he would feel hurt and betrayed.

Kai plopped his fishing line into the pond and took a seat on a round, gray rock. Sammy joined him, eyeing the smaller fish zipping around the water. He licked his lips and dipped his fin into the water. The next moment he slipped all the way in.

SPLASH!

"Maybe don't scare away all the fish," Kai laughed.

"Aha!" exclaimed Bion. He pulled a leather-bound book from the backpack.

Delphi scrunched her nose as Bion flipped through the pages.

Bion landed on a page called "Artemis" and showed Delphi a picture of mermaids with streaked hair. There were other animals scattered on the page as well.

"Aunt Cora has a book just like this," Delphi mumbled. She moved her face closer to a picture of a sea lion, but Bion snapped the book shut.

"You know Aunt Cora?" Bion asked.

"Yes, she raised me," Delphi said. "*You* know Aunt Cora?" A small drop of water hit her forehead as the sky rumbled.

Bion adjusted his glasses. "Why, yes, yes I do. A lovely lady. I've worked with her quite a few times with creatures. Sometimes she keeps them for me when I run out of room." A large drop of rain hit his glasses. And within a few seconds, it began to pour.

"But we must be going. We have to get this food back to the others," Bion shouted over the hard thud of the downpour. "It was nice to meet you. Do tell Cora and Poseidon that Bion and Willow said hello."

Before Delphi could say anything, Bion was gone.

Willow waved before following her father out. Her orange hair was now dripping wet. "The entrance is on the other side of those bushes with red berries," Willow explained. "On the cliff, you will see a carving of a purple *house*." Willow laughed. "Not a purple horse or hose."

"Thanks, Willow!" Kai said with a big wave and a shiver. It sure was getting chilly.

"Come back anytime! And just leave the rod when you're done," Willow said with one last wave before bolting off.

Delphi slumped down beside Kai. Both of their clothes were wet and clinging to them like plastic wrap. But Delphi hardly seemed to notice the rain.

"What was that about?" Kai asked.

The sound of thunder boomed over the pond.

Delphi groaned. "Oh, just Aunt Cora keeping things from me. Again!" Delphi's shoulders slumped. "Aunt Cora has the exact same book that Bion does. It's the same book that she showed you when you first got your trident necklace. So why wouldn't she tell me that I was in there? Why is she hiding things?"

"Delphi, I'm sure anything Aunt Cora has hidden from you was to protect you. She loves you."

"I think it's time," Delphi said.

"Time for what?" Kai asked. "To go live with the mermaids?"

The loud thunder rumbled through the air once more.

Kai swallowed the lump in his throat. Thoughts of the mermaid world swirled through his mind. Seahorse races and seashell homes were just two of the highlights. He could see why Delphi would want to spend more time there. She deserved to know where she came from. But he didn't like the idea of his friend not being around to be a Protector with him.

"No, look at your rod!" Delphi exclaimed.

The tip of Kai's rod pointed straight down. He had a big bite. He whipped the rod the other way to hook his catch. Delphi helped him pull in the line. The shimmery fish flip-flopped all the way to shore.

Kai unhooked the fish. He wasn't expecting the fish to be stinkier fresh. And he wasn't expecting it to have such powerful tails.

WHAP!

One of its tails slapped Kai's hand, running a sharp barb right into his skin.

"Ouch!" Kai yelped. He dropped the fish in pain. He looked down, trying to see where it went. The rain streaming into his eyes made everything a blur.

"The fish!" Delphi cried. She dove on the ground to try to grab it, but it was too late.

PLOP!

The fish jumped back into the shallow pond.

SPLASH!

Delphi jumped in after it. The water came only to her knees.

"I can still see it!" Delphi called to Kai. "We can corner it if you jump in."

SPLASH! Splash!

Both Kai and Sammy jumped into the pond. The fish's glimmering scales looked like a piece of red sunlight underwater, making it easy to follow. They chased the fish to the edge of the pond, cornering it against a smooth rock. Kai reached down and scooped it up—being very careful of its tail this time.

"We did it!" Delphi cheered. The rain slowed down and came to a stop.

Kai looked up at the gray clouds. "Too bad it couldn't have stopped a couple minutes ago.

I guess Mother Nature doesn't know we're in a rush."

Delphi laughed.

Now they just had to get to that entrance and get that compass.

They waded through the red berry bushes, and the entrance was right where Willow had said. And etched onto the mountain was a carving of a purple house.

The windows of the house were made with two tridents, their prongs touching. Kai and Delphi both slid off their necklaces and placed them in the shapes. With a click, the door opened.

CHAPTER 8

CHASING WATERFALLS

Kai, Delphi, and Sammy zigzagged through the rocky tunnels inside the mountain. The only sounds were their footsteps and Sammy flip-flopping along behind them. The air was heavy and warm. Even after being in that chilly rain shower, Kai was roasting after only a few minutes of walking.

Just as Kai wiped a bead of sweat off his forehead, a cherry-sized ball of light appeared at the end of the tunnel. Soon it grew into an orange, then a watermelon, then a pumpkin. By the time they reached it, it was taller than a giraffe.

The sound of rushing water overpowered

their footsteps as they walked into the opening. They stepped into a large room with rocky walls and a waterfall. It wasn't just any waterfall, though. The water was smooth as glass, reflecting the space as clearly as a mirror.

Kai went to stick his hand in the waterfall, but the warm water was too powerful to push through.

"Where do we go now?" Delphi asked.

"Not through that water," Kai answered. "It is way too strong." That was when he noticed a riddle carved into the opposite wall. "But look!"

"Find what is different to see the light. Match what is wet to all in sight," Delphi read out loud.

"What do you think that means?" Kai asked. He was okay at puzzles but nowhere near as good as Delphi.

Delphi read the words a few more times and looked around the room.

"Hmm, what we need to find is different, wet, and easy to see?"

Kai gazed around the room. There was a huge log in one corner and a pile of stones in the other. The floor was mostly dirt, but a few colored rocks were scattered about. Then there was a small pool under the waterfall.

"These colored rocks are different and easy

to see," Kai said as he plucked a green one off the ground.

"That's true!" said Delphi. "Maybe we just need to wet them."

They collected the rainbow of rocks and wet them in the pool. A loud sound erupted from the log behind them.

They whirled around, hoping for a door to open. But instead, they found Sammy lying belly-up, snoring on the log.

"Sammy!" Delphi and Kai both laughed.

"I don't think that did anything," Delphi said. "Unless putting Sammy to sleep counts." She turned around to look at the room once more.

Kai exhaled loudly as he took the last of the rocks out of the water. He tried pushing one into the waterfall, but it was still too powerful.

He circled the room once more, taking note of everything in it. He didn't understand what the riddle was talking about.

"I don't think we are ever going to get this!" Kai complained. "Pineapple Cove will be ruined and it's all because we couldn't solve this riddle."

"Have patience," Delphi said as she ran her hand over the log. "Sometimes riddles take time."

"We don't have a lot of time," Kai mumbled. He took another lap of the room. It didn't matter how many times he circled the space, though. He couldn't spot anything different, wet, and easy to see. He just kept coming back to the powerful waterfall, and it didn't seem like it was any help.

He glanced at the glossy surface of the waterfall to see if Delphi was having any luck, but she was gone, and so was Sammy.

Kai spun around in a panic. Sammy was still napping on the log, and Delphi was looking at the pile of stones in the corner. Kai was also missing from the reflection.

"Delphi, come look at this. Things are missing from the reflection in this waterfall."

Delphi came over and examined the reflection. "You're right! There are also things that aren't in the same place as the reflection. I think we need to move stuff around to match the waterfall. But first, we need to find what is different."

They picked the gems off the floor and lined them up on the log like the colors of the rainbow. Next, they stacked the stones like a pyramid. Lastly, they had to match the two-tail fish that was swimming in the pool under the waterfall.

There was one problem, though—the two-tail fish swimming under the waterfall was alive. And theirs wasn't.

CHAPTER 9

RAINBOW TUNNELS

Delphi and Kai watched as the two-tail fish in the reflection swam around. They needed to match the waterfall's reflection. But Kai doubted that was possible now.

"We don't have time for a new fish," Kai said. "So we have to try."

He dropped the fish in the pool. It floated to the top for a few seconds, but then its two tails started wiggling. The fish came alive and started mirroring the waterfall fish.

Kai and Delphi cheered.

"Everything is exactly where it should be," Delphi said. "Now something should happen."

Everyone froze as they waited. But nothing

changed. Sammy flipped over to watch the swimming fish. He licked his lips.

"I don't get it," Kai said after a minute. "Everything is exactly the same."

"Wait! Not everything," Delphi said. "We aren't in the reflection. We have to hide."

Kai and Delphi crouched behind the large log.

"Sammy!" Delphi called. "Stop watching that fish and get over here." Sammy did so. As soon as he got behind the log, the waterfall fell with a *WHOOSH!*

A small room appeared and right in the center was a gold compass. Kai ran over and took the compass from the pedestal. The metal felt cold in his hand. He flipped it open to see which way it was pointing. But the dial didn't move at all. No matter which way Kai faced, it just pointed in front of him.

"This must be why we have to take it to Cybil," Kai said. The staircase was right behind the pedestal, and they began their climb.

Kai was sweaty and out of breath by the time they reached the top. He thought they must have climbed a thousand stairs. He tilted his head back, taking a huge inhale of fresh air. Next, he turned his attention to the top of the mountain.

The stairs had led them to the very peak, with a circle filled with rainbow rocks. The edge of this colorful circle was lined with tall trees. And in the center, there was a glass case with an empty black box inside. A man with a turtle shell was hunched over beside the case. He shook his head as he looked at the case. Then he grabbed the box.

"Happy to see you, young Protectors. I am Cybil," the turtle man said. "Hand the compass over. I shall give it the power to guide the way to the egg. I know you have no time to spare."

Before Kai could decide whether or not to trust Cybil, the compass was floating out of his hand. It flew right over and hit Cybil's palm with a small slap.

Kai and Delphi glanced at each other with wide eyes.

"And you must be Kai and Delphi," Cybil said as he inspected the compass.

"Aarf," said Sammy.

"And Sammy," Cybil said with a crooked smile.

Cybil walked the compass to a large, black cauldron sitting over the fire. There was a wisp of steam squiggling on top of it like a snake. Kai's gaze followed the smoke stream up, just in time to see the lightning whizzing across the sky. Only three more lightning bolts.

Kai shifted his feet. His stomach grew squirmy, and his heartbeat quickened.

"Couldn't this have been done to the compass before we got here?" Kai asked. "We're kind of in a rush."

"This shall only take a minute," Cybil assured Kai. "Patience is key, and this can only be done with a Protector. Can I see your necklace?"

Kai slipped the chain that held the trident over his head and handed it to Cybil. The smell of the potion made him wrinkle his nose. He knew that smell. It was the same stench that the blue fruit had given off in the empty village. He quickly backed away, trying not to gag.

Cybil dangled the trident over the hot cauldron. Kai was afraid he would drop it in, but instead, he dripped a blue liquid down it.

Cybil dunked the compass in the potion and held it out to the sky after muttering a few words.

"May this guide you to what you seek," Cybil said as he handed the trident and compass back to Kai. Then he gave a black velvet box to Delphi. "The egg must be put back in here before the last lightning strike to seal the crack. Good luck."

Delphi and Kai opened the compass, which now smelled like spoiled milk. The needle was pointing down, which meant they had to get off of Turtle Mountain.

Delphi looked over the edge of the mountain. An ocean of sky circled them with no other land in sight.

"With no ship, how are we supposed to get down?" Delphi asked.

"Take the slides," Cybil said. "It is the fastest way off the mountain during lockdown. You will know the way, Delphi."

He pointed to an opening beside the one that they had come from.

Delphi turned to the opening. "How will I know the way?" she asked. But Cybil was already gone.

They went in the opening Cybil had indicated, and it forked off into three tunnels. Purple, blue, and green.

"Which way do we go?" Kai asked.

Delphi shrugged. "How am I supposed to know?"

"Cybil said you would, and Turtle People are supposed to be very smart."

Delphi's eyes trailed across the tunnels. "Wait, this looks familiar." She pointed to a small, black mark that looked like a turtle. It was right on top of the three tunnels.

"Aunt Cora used to read me a story about rainbow tunnels as a little girl," Delphi said. "It was one of my favorites, and I knew it by heart.

But I always thought it was just a story. I remember the pictures had that little turtle mark though… so maybe it wasn't just a story." Delphi clenched her eyes shut. "Hold on, maybe I can still remember."

After a minute, Kai began to get squirmy. "Delphi, we don't have a lot of time. Maybe we should just pick a tunnel."

"No, I've got this," Delphi said.

"Through the green tunnel, you will find a waterslide that's one-of-a-kind. Take a left, then hang a right. Slide right down, hang on tight!"

They made their way through the green tunnel and soon found themselves following a small river. The small stream of water flowed to a round opening in a wall encrusted with orange gems.

"This is it!" Delphi declared. "Come on, guys!" She enthusiastically flung herself through the round opening. She disappeared and Sammy dove after her, followed by Kai.

"Yippee!" Kai shouted as he slid through the hole. The warm stream of water sloshed against him as he zoomed down the water slide. It spiraled downward like a tornado, always curving to the right. His view started off as gem-covered ceilings, but soon the sides of the slide became clear. He could see the whole island!

There were all the shops that Bob the Blob had accidentally destroyed when kidnapping Kai's mom and sister. They now looked good as new, with freshly painted shutters and all the holes repaired. He could hear the town bell chiming in the distance. Then there was the sandy beach not far from where he had saved Blue the dolphin. Kai tried to spot his own home, but he was speeding down the slide too fast to get a good view.

They popped out in a small pond not far from Aunt Cora's house. As soon as they exited, the bush magically grew thicker, hiding the opening of the slide.

"That was awesome," Kai said. "But we have to find Hobbs now and follow the compass. We are running out of time. If we don't get there soon, the sun will be gone forever and Pineapple Cove will be doomed."

CHAPTER 10
OLD FRIENDS

Delphi and Kai took off their shoes and raced down the beach. Even though the sun was behind the gray clouds, the sand still felt warm squidging between their toes. Kai patted his pocket to make sure the compass was secure.

It wasn't long before Aunt Cora's house came into view. It was rickety and twisty and three stories high. They followed the seashell path to the front porch, but just before they got inside, a strange sound came from the sky.

Squeak. Whoosh. Whoosh. Squeak.

"What's that sound?" asked Kai. He looked around but couldn't find where it was coming from.

SQUEAK. WHOOSH. WHOOSH. SQUEAK.

The sound got louder and the sky began to darken.

SQUEAK! WHOOSH! WHOOSH! SQUEAK!

Aunt Cora ran out of the house, her blue skirt swishing like the ocean. Hobbs wasn't far behind. And with him, he had the Storm Blaster.

A large engine-powered blimp descended from the cloud above. The plump, red balloon had "JKS" scrawled in gold writing.

Hobbs' face went white as a ghost. "It can't be!" He shoved the Storm Blaster at Kai and Delphi. "Take this and don't let it out of your sight," he commanded. Kai gladly grabbed the blaster. He didn't feel like a true Protector on Turtle Mountain without it.

A man with inky black hair poked his head over the edge of the blimp. He had a pointy beard and a sly smile. A crow was perched on his shoulder but soon flew away.

A deep voice boomed from the blimp, "Hobbs, we meet again!"

"Jasper," Hobbs growled. "I should have known you were still lurking around."

Jasper laughed. "Oh, my old friend. I have been doing more than lurking." Jasper pulled an egg-shaped object from his pocket. The glass caught the light and lit up like a small ball of fire.

Kai's heart stopped. He had never seen the crystal egg before, but he knew that was it.

"Give that back right now!" yelled Kai. "That belongs on Turtle Mountain."

Jasper let out a roaring laugh that echoed over the beach. "And why would I do that?"

Kai hid the blaster behind his back. "Because if you don't, we are going to take it!" he shouted.

"And how do you expect to do that?" Jasper

taunted. "Once I fly out of here, you will never find me."

Kai reached into his pocket and pulled out the shiny compass. "With this!"

"Don't, Kai!" Aunt Cora warned. "It's a trick." But it was too late.

SWOOP!

Just as soon as Kai put the compass in his hand, it was plucked out. The black bird swooped down and nabbed it. The bird flew back up to the blimp and dropped the compass in Jasper's hands.

"Ah, thank you, Persil," Jasper cooed. "I was hoping to not have to come here, but you blasted kids found the compass. Even after Persil took the fish. Oh well, guess it doesn't matter now."

Jasper cackled, and the blimp began to lift high into the clouds once more. "See you once I am King of the Sea!"

The blimp headed toward the ocean.

SQUEAK! WHOOSH! WHOOSH! SQUEAK!

Hobbs sprinted to the blimp and leaped toward the hanging rope ladder. He grasped the bottom rung with his left hand.

Kai and Delphi raced after Hobbs, trying to also jump at the ladder. But their shorter legs meant they couldn't get high enough. Sammy didn't have the same problem. He sprang like he was jumping on a gum tree. He grabbed Hobbs' pants with his teeth and was lifted into the air.

"Sammy!" Delphi cried.

"Cora, you need to tell them the secret!" Hobbs yelled back. "I don't think I can do this on my own. You need to tell them the secret to find me and the crystal egg. And hurry!"

Lightning zipped across the sky as the blimp flew to a spot down the beach. This was their chance. Kai and Delphi continued running, trying to jump on the blimp while it was low. But as soon as the blimp landed by the water, the beach swallowed it like quicksand. Hobbs, Sammy, and the crystal egg were gone. And only two more bolts of lightning were left before their home was ruined forever.

CHAPTER 11
SECRETS

Kai and Delphi ran into the house. Aunt Cora was plopping Finley the fish in a smaller bowl. He smiled his sharp-toothed grin.

"So what is the big secret?" Delphi hissed at Cora.

"I'll explain along the way," Cora answered.

They raced out of the house with Finley in hand and made their way down the beach. Kai recognized this area well, as he often collected clams here. Angry waves were slamming against the shore.

When Aunt Cora didn't say anything, Delphi spoke again. "So first, you didn't tell me I was a mermaid. Then you didn't tell me the rainbow tunnels were real. Now what?"

"Oh, my little starfish, I never kept the rainbow tunnels on Turtle Mountain from you," Cora responded. "Don't you remember the story I read to you as a little girl? It was your favorite!"

"Of course, I do," Delphi said. "It's how we got down. But until then I just thought they were a story. And what if I didn't remember? Kai and I could still be stuck up there."

"But you did remember," Cora said.

Kai gave Finley a wave, and Finley waved back, as he always did.

"Is a book like that how you know where you're going now?" Kai asked.

"I wish!" said Aunt Cora, walking faster. "But I have no idea where we are going."

Kai stopped. "Then why are we following you?"

Aunt Cora held up the fishbowl. "You aren't

following me; you're following Finley."

"We're following a fish?" Kai scoffed. "Great, we're doomed!" He looked into the fishbowl. "No offense, Finley." Finley blew a bubble.

"I'm with Kai on this," Delphi said. "How can a fish help find a crystal egg?"

"Because Finley isn't just any fish—he's Poseidon, King of the Sea."

Kai's breath caught in his throat, and he came to a stop. "He's who!?"

"Finley is Poseidon?!" Delphi gasped.

Pit-pat-pit-pat. Kai's heart began to race. It couldn't be. He had been waiting and waiting to meet Poseidon. To get some sort of letter or a call. Anything from Poseidon himself. Now, Aunt Cora said the fish he passed so often was Poseidon, the King of the Sea? He didn't believe it.

He caught up to Cora and glared at the fish in the tank. But upon looking closer at Finley, his gaze softened. Right on Finley's tail was a tiny mark of Poseidon—a trident. Maybe Finley *was* Poseidon.

"Why would you have Poseidon?" Kai finally asked. "And why is he a fish?"

"We have to keep going," Aunt Cora said. "I'll explain more later. But you must tell no one. Especially not Jasper. You heard him: he wants to be the new King of the Sea."

"But why?" Kai asked.

"And how?" Delphi asked.

Cora shrugged. "If I only knew." She stopped at a spot behind a rock where Kai had hid his clam bucket. "Poseidon says this is the way."

"Oh, now you can talk to fish?" Delphi scoffed.

"No, not exactly," Cora said. "But I do understand his body language a little. I think Jasper is going to his secret lair and Poseidon knows the way."

"But this is just a rock," Delphi said.

Beside the rock was a big square outline poking out of the sand. Kai often threw his bucket here but never paid much attention. He swept away the sand with his fingers and revealed a wooden hatch.

With a big tug, the hatch popped open. A wooden ladder led to an underground tunnel.

Drip. Drop. Drip. Drop.

Water dribbled from the ceiling and slowly streamed down the scribbly walls. The swirly scribbles glowed blue when the light shone on them.

They walked quickly through the moist tunnel in silence. Delphi stomped along behind Kai and Aunt Cora.

"These must be the old pirate tunnels," Cora said. "I've read about them but never found one myself."

A blue-and-gold light danced at the end of

the tunnel. As they got closer, it got brighter, and the smell of salt got stronger. It led to a room with a large pool. The pool was lined in gold coins, making all the water shimmer. Except for one side of the pool, where there was an underwater tunnel.

"That must be the way," Kai said. "What do you think, Finley—err, Mr. Poseidon, sir?"

He looked at Finley, who swam in a circle. "Blink twice if that is the way."

Finely didn't blink.

"I don't think this is the way," Kai said.

Delphi shook her head. "Fish don't have eyelids, so they can't blink."

"Oh," said Kai. "Um, swim up and down if this is the right way." To Kai's delight, Poseidon swam up, then down. It was the right way!

SPLASH!

Kai dove into the pool, ready to swim.

"Wait, we need helmets," Cora said. "We don't know how long that tunnel goes underwater."

Kai hadn't thought of that. He looked at Delphi with her arms crossed behind Cora.

"Delphi, I bet you can do it!" Kai said as he pulled himself out of the pool.

"Me?" Delphi uncrossed her arms and looked down at the water. She shivered.

"Why me?"

"Well, mermaids can breathe underwater. You're part mermaid, so you should at least be able to hold your breath a long time," Kai answered. "Remember at the beach when you held your breath for five minutes the other day? Most people can't do that!"

Delphi smiled. "I could have held it longer, but a fish touched my foot and scared me."

"Exactly," said Kai. "You've got this!"

Cora gave Delphi a smile and a nod.

SPLASH!

Delphi took a deep breath, dove into the water, and swam through the underwater tunnel.

Kai twisted his hands as he waited. He wondered if he should have gone himself. Luckily, it wasn't long before Delphi swam back up from the tunnel.

She surfaced in the water. "The tunnel is short and leads to an air bubble," she said.

"Blue was snacking on fish right outside, so I asked him to bring us helmets." She dove back under.

Splash.

With one small splash, Cora dumped Poseidon into the pool.

SPLASH! SPLASH!

Kai and Cora followed.

CHAPTER 12
CRYSTALS OF THE SEA

Kai, Delphi, and Aunt Cora were in the giant bubble under the ocean. Poseidon was just outside, swimming in the water.

Kai peered out the side of the bubble and watched a school of fish zip by. Their scales glimmered a mix of orange and yellow. They looked like giant goldfish. Kai held his breath and popped his head out of the bubble to get a better look.

BLOOP!

The saltwater instantly stung his eyes and everything became a blur. Kai quickly pulled himself back into the bubble.

"We will definitely need some sort of

helmets," Kai said. He rubbed his eyes. "How did you see in this water?" he asked Delphi.

"The saltwater doesn't seem to bother me," Delphi said.

Kai rubbed his eyes again. "Lucky."

With a clickity-chirp, Blue swam to the bubble, toting a net filled with three glass helmets. He gently poked each helmet through the bubble. Delphi, Kai, and Aunt Cora put on their helmets.

"Alright," Cora said, "let's go."

Aunt Cora gave the delivery dolphin a pat on the head. "Get Hermes and send him to my house." Blue took off with a chirp and a tail flick.

The trio dipped and dived through slimy seaweed in silence. Poseidon swam at the front of the group. Eventually, they reached a large gray rock with a carving that looked like a blob with ten legs. Poseidon came to a stop and looked around anxiously. Then he turned toward Cora and stared.

"Oh dear," said Cora. "I think he's lost."

"How is the King of the Sea lost?" Kai asked.

"Finley fish are known to have a hard time seeing in darker water. That could be part of it," Cora said.

"This is a disaster," said Delphi. She sat down on the sandy ocean floor and looked toward the surface of the water. Yellow fish with black spots floated not too far overhead.

"Ow," yelped Delphi. Something sharp was poking her bottom. She yanked it out, expecting a shell. Instead, she found a macaroni-sized crystal.

The glitter of the crystal caught Kai's eye.

"Where did you find that?" Kai asked.

Delphi stood up and rubbed her bottom. "In the sand."

Kai looked around the sandy ocean floor and noticed more crystals. There was a whole trail.

"These are just like the crystals Captain Hobbs has," Kai explained, remembering the crystals that Hobbs always carried in his pocket. A small bag flapping on a piece of seaweed grabbed Kai's attention. It was a small pouch with the name "Hobbs" stitched on it.

"Wait, these don't just look like Hobbs' crystals; they *are* his!" Kai exclaimed. "I bet if we follow them, we can find him, Sammy, and the crystal egg!"

They swam as fast as their feet and fins could take them. The trail led them to a large boulder with a dark opening, where the trail disappeared. Kai peered into it, trying to make out any shapes. All he saw was blackness.

Kai gripped the Storm Blaster in his hand and got ready to go through the opening. Just then, two beady eyes popped out, followed by a leg that was longer than Kai. The giant crab, with its bumpy orange skin, stepped out of the rock. It stretched out each of its five-foot-long legs. It was much bigger than any crab Kai had ever seen on the beach. It was a monster crab!

Kai quickly aimed his blaster at it.

"From the oceans cold and warm, I summon Poseidon's storm." Kai gave the blaster a single pump. The swirling water blasted out of the nozzle and zipped by the crab's head.

"He's going to eat us!" Kai cried. Everyone swam to take shelter behind the big rock, but the crab didn't follow. Instead, it slurped the crystals off the ocean floor.

"Wait, I don't think he wants anything to do with us," said Delphi. "He seems to just want to eat those crystals." The crab then sucked up a slimy plant out of the sand. "And anything else in the sand."

"That's right," said Aunt Cora. "Spider crabs around here are bottom feeders that like to eat what they can find in the sand. And they just love crystals of the sea."

"Crystals of the sea?" Kai asked.

"They're a sign of friendship and gratitude,"

Cora answered. "They are also rumored to be a form of protection. But mostly, they're a tasty snack for the spider crabs. We should follow the trail before the spider crab licks them all up."

They followed the crystal trail to a jagged rock sitting on the ocean floor. But it wasn't just any rock—it was a secret castle. Or at least that was what the front door told them. Wedged between two pointy peaks that looked like upside-down ice cream cones was a warped wooden door. A sign hung from it with drippy, painted letters that read *SECRET CASTLE. KEEP OUT!*

Kai swam closer to get a better look and quickly noticed the door was fake. It was painted on, and not very well. Whoever painted it couldn't even keep paint in the lines. He lightly ran his hand over the round, hairy plants sprouting from the cracks in the rock.

"Ouch!" Kai cried. They were much more

pokey than he had thought. The colorful fish didn't seem to mind, though. They zipped around, weaving in and out of the plants and rocks. It didn't take long for Poseidon to join them.

After circling the castle for what felt like

forever, Poseidon led them to a wooden door covered in pink coral on the side of the castle. This time it was a real door with a door handle and everything. And to the left, there was a rusty lock. Kai tried to push the door, but it wouldn't budge. A glimmer of gold caught Kai's eye. It was metallic writing.

Rearrange my letters to find the key
DERUN HET RENGE ROLAC

"It looks like an anagram," Delphi said. Kai wasn't surprised she knew about this type of puzzle. After all, Delphi loved puzzles and did them all the time with Aunt Cora.

"What's an 'anagram'?" Kai questioned.

"You have to rearrange the letters in each word to get the right answer," Cora answered.

After a couple minutes, they got the first three words.

"Under the green... what's the last word?" Kai mumbled.

"Coral!" Delphi exclaimed. "Under the green coral!" She whipped her head around, and an emerald patch caught her eye. Delphi swam over and gently tipped the piece of coral over. There was a golden key underneath. It fit right into the lock, and the wood door creaked open.

After swimming down a short hallway, they surfaced in a room with air. Kai took off his helmet and took a deep breath. It smelled stale in this room, kind of like wet socks. On the walls were colorful murals of fish and mermaids. This place sure was fishy—and it wasn't just the decor.

Delphi placed Poseidon back in the bowl just as Hobbs came running out of an arched stone doorway. He was huffing and puffing so much that he was hard to understand.

"We need to go now," Hobbs said. He took in a deep breath. "Follow me." He ran back the way he had come. Kai, Delphi, and Cora followed. A bamboo cage fell on top of them as soon as they entered the next room. They were trapped!

Jasper's evil laugh echoed through the gray brick chamber. The windows all had swirling bars. There was a round pool filled with water sitting in the middle of the room. But it wasn't fancy like the pirate tunnel pool. It was a kid's blow-up pool with rubber ducks on the side. It looked funny with the fancy crystal chandelier on the ceiling.

"Thank you, Hobbs," Jasper said.

"What are you doing?" Kai said as he tried to tug the bars loose. "Let us out!" Through the skylight in the room, a bolt of lightning was visible. Only one bolt was left.

A small whimper came from the cage beside them.

"Sammy!" Delphi cried with relief.

Jasper tented his fingers as he took a seat on a wooden throne lined with red velvet. Persil sat on a smaller throne next to him. A smile tugged at Jasper's lips.

Kai raised the blaster, ready to cool down Jasper. "From the oceans cold and warm—"

But before he could finish, Hobbs walked over and yanked it from his hands.

"Hobbs works for me now," Jasper said. "Toss it!"

Hobbs chucked the blaster to the side of the room. It hit the floor with a loud thud.

CHAPTER 13
UNDER A SPELL

"NOOOOO!" yelled Kai as he watched the blaster hit the corner of the floor. He didn't understand why Hobbs would do that. It was like he was under a spell. Kai stared at the blaster.

At least it doesn't look broken, he thought.

With a smile, Jasper grabbed the egg from his pocket. "In just a short time, Pineapple Cove will go dark forever. And I will become King of the Sea."

"Why would *you* become King of the Sea?" Kai asked.

"Why wouldn't I?" Jasper answered. "Poseidon is nowhere to be found. Once the power of light is gone from the crystal egg, the whole island will be dark. After that happens, I can dress like Poseidon and fool everybody. It is much easier to fool people in the dark. Although, I think my costume is pretty good!"

Jasper stood up and slipped on a wig made from a blue mop head. Then he picked up a trident made with the mop handle, duct tape, and spaghetti noodles. It might not have been bad if the spaghetti noodles weren't cooked. They looked like pale, wiggly worms.

"It's like we're twins!" Jasper said. "What do you think?"

Kai had to hold back a laugh. He had never seen Poseidon in human form, but he was sure he didn't look like that.

"You do realize that there will be no Pineapple Cove if you don't give back the egg," Aunt Cora clucked.

"Sure, there will be," Jasper said. "The sun

will be gone, but we can use light bulbs."

"That's not how it works," Kai said. "Without the sun, our food and plants wouldn't grow. Without the sun, it would be too cold to live for the animals, fish, and townsfolk. Without the sun, Pineapple Cove is doomed."

Kai could have sworn he saw Hobbs smile out of the corner of his eye. However, Jasper certainly wasn't smiling anymore.

"But, but," stuttered Jasper. "Arg!" he screamed in frustration. "You kids are ruining everything! First, there was the octopus you stopped. Then there was Amphi, the Queen of Sirenia. Do you know how hard it is to get an octopus to drink a potion? Oh, but I figured it out. One saucy fish dinner later and he was under my spell."

Jasper stopped and frowned. "But then the octopus just wanted to play with all the boats. He was supposed to attack the island and get the people to turn on Poseidon. After all, shouldn't a good King of the Sea be able to control the sea creatures? Then I could have been elected as the new King of the Sea."

"You put the octopus and Amphi under a spell?" Kai gasped.

"Yes!" Jasper sneered. "I knew after the octopus that I had to get rid of that Storm Blaster. So I put a potion in Amphi's sea-cherry fizzer. She was supposed to get the blaster, but you foiled my plan again. At least it distracted you long enough so I could steal the crystal egg." Jasper turned the egg over in his hand.

Kai's blood began to boil. He remembered the octopus that had threatened his home. And his mom and sister getting kidnapped.

"And then what?" Kai challenged. "The whole island goes black. No one will be able to live on Pineapple Cove anymore, so you will be King of Nothing."

Jasper frowned. "I haven't thought that far. Maybe I will— Maybe I will… um, fix the sun."

This time Kai knew he saw Hobbs smile. He turned to Hobbs, who gave him a wink. Hobbs pulled the sea crystals out of his pocket.

Of course! Kai thought. *The crystals must have protected him from Jasper's spell.*

"I think it's time to get rid of you once and for all," Jasper said.

Jasper stood up from his throne. He carefully put the egg on the velvet seat cushion before he walked over to the kiddie pool.

Hobbs made a duck-beak motion with his hand. Kai knew what that meant—they had to keep Jasper talking.

"Um, why do you have a kiddie pool?" Kai asked.

Jasper groaned. "Look, I'm on a tight budget. Being a villain is expensive. Do you know how much those nice pools cost?"

Kai, Delphi, and Cora watched as Hobbs snuck to the chair and snatched the egg.

Kai couldn't contain his smile. "No, how much?"

Jasper's face got red. "Well, I don't know exactly how much. But a lot!"

"Caw! Caw!" called Persil.

Jasper hushed the bird. Then he dropped a pinch of green flakes from a small vial into the pool. The pool began to swirl.

Slish. Slosh.

Jasper skipped back to his throne. "Once I am King of the Sea and form Jasper's Guardians, I will make sure not to let any silly kids on my team."

"Caw! Caw!" called Persil again.

Jasper plopped down and then jumped to his feet. He looked at the red velvet of his throne. Then under it, then around it.

"Where is the crystal egg?" he bellowed. He

turned around and saw Hobbs holding it in one hand with a sly smile.

"Persil! Why didn't you tell me?" Jasper hissed. Persil rolled his eyes. The duck pool began to swirl harder.

SLISH! SLOOSH! SLISH! SLOOSH!

Jasper lurched toward Hobbs.

"Put it in the velvet box, quick!" Hobbs said. Kai knew he was talking about the box that Cybil had given Delphi on Turtle Mountain.

Hobbs tossed the egg toward the cage. It sailed through the air toward Kai. The egg grazed his fingertips. But then it flew the opposite direction.

The duck pool was creating a vortex. And the whole room was being sucked toward it.

CHAPTER 14
WHIRLPOOL

SLISH! SLOOSH! SLISH! SLOOSH!

The whirlpool was beginning to pull harder. Kai watched the vortex swallow the crystal egg. Next, the bamboo cage flew toward it. Then the whirlpool ate the storm blaster for dessert. Everyone else was next.

Kai grabbed onto the bars on the nearby window with Cora and Delphi. Aunt Cora was holding Poseidon in one hand. Sammy was still in his cage.

SLISH! SLOOSH! SLISH! SLOOSH!

The suction was beginning to be too much. The thrones squealed on the stone floor as they dragged closer to the whirlpool.

Kai thought of their long journey to get here and couldn't believe it was ending like this. They had dodged slime cannons, hopped on clouds, slid down rainbow slides, and discovered the secret pirate tunnel. But it wasn't enough.

Suddenly, Kai remembered fishing on Turtle Mountain and the small whirlpool. Would the trick that Bion and Willow had used work here?

"Shush the whirlpool," he yelled.

"Good idea!" Delphi agreed.

"Shh!" Kai and Delphi started. But nothing seemed to be happening.

"On no!" cried Cora. The fishbowl slipped from her hand and flew into the pool.

"Poseidon!" Kai screamed.

Hobbs, Jasper, and Persil were holding on to a window on the other side of the room.

Jasper smirked. "That was Poseidon? Now I know where he has been hiding all this time!"

"Kai, my hands are starting to slip," Delphi cried.

"Try shushing again," Kai said.

Kai and Delphi started shushing. This time Cora and Hobbs joined in. The powerful suction got slower, but not before sucking in a bit more. Cora was tugged from the bars of the window and flew straight into the small pool. Persil wasn't far behind.

"Aunt Cora!" Delphi cried, trying to catch her hand.

"Persil!" yelled Jasper. Persil was the last thing to be sucked into the pool before it stopped.

Delphi raced to the pool to search the water. She sloshed her hands in it and patted everywhere, but nothing was there. It looked just like a normal kid's pool.

"Where is she?" Delphi cried. "Where did it take her!?"

"Give it a second," Jasper said, breathing heavily.

The pool made a loud sloshing sound. And within a second, it spat up a huge gush of water and everything it had sucked in.

The crystal egg, blaster, and Poseidon launched into the air, along with other bits and bobs from around the room. The mess hung in the air for a moment, and then began falling toward the ground.

Kai looked to Delphi, but her attention was still on the pool. He turned to Hobbs next. Hobbs was right under Poseidon. Kai knew he could only catch one thing. While the blaster had helped them a lot, he knew it had to be the crystal egg. He lunged for the egg and caught it. It was slick and slippery in his hands. The blaster slammed to the ground, snapping in half.

Kai felt his stomach drop. Then, the pool launched something else in Kai's direction. A passed-out Persil flew through the air, and he was about to hit the ground.

Kai outstretched one of his arms and dove for the bird. He reached for the clump of wet, black feathers and grabbed him just in time. He saved the bird from the hard stone, but he wished he could say the same about the crystal egg.

The egg popped out of his other hand on the dive down and smashed on the floor. The crystal egg was in a million little pieces. The blaster

was broken. It seemed the only one who made a good catch was Captain Hobbs with Poseidon.

"Persil?" said Jasper, looking at the ruffled black bird. "Persil!?"

Jasper raced to the bird, who was still lying

motionless in Kai's hand. He didn't even seem to care that the egg was smashed. He scooped up Persil. "I'm so sorry!" he wailed.

Water gushed out of Persil's beak like a small fountain. He hopped back to his feet.

"Thank goodness!" said Jasper with a sigh of relief. The bird flapped to Jasper's shoulder, water spraying off his wings.

"Caw! Caw!" cried Persil.

"Alright, maybe the whirlpool wasn't the best plan," Jasper admitted. "I didn't believe the spell book when it said it would be that strong."

"Jasper," said Hobbs. "You're going to have to come with me."

Jasper's face turned pale. "Or not." He sprinted out of the room. Hobbs followed. But not before plopping Poseidon in the ducky pool.

Kai looked down at Delphi, who was kneeling by the pool. The pool had spat out everything—everything except for Aunt Cora.

Sammy flippered over and licked the tears streaming down Delphi's cheeks.

"What if I never get her back, Kai?" Delphi wept. "I've been so mad at her lately, but she is the only family I have. I know she loves me. It's just been hard not to know who I am. I wish she would have told me."

Kai hugged Delphi as she began to cry harder.

"I do love you," came a voice from above. "And I only kept things from you to protect you. I would never want to hurt you."

Kai and Delphi whipped their heads toward the ceiling. Aunt Cora was hanging from the chandelier—the whirlpool had spit her out after all.

Cora climbed down from the chandelier and gave Delphi a hug.

"We have a lot to talk about," Cora said. "But I've always loved you and always will."

Delphi sniffled. "I love you too."

The last bolt of lightning flashed across the sky above. Its light shimmered in the broken piece of the crystal egg.

CHAPTER 15
NEXT MISSION

Kai, Delphi, and Cora sat on the beach and watched the sunset. Poseidon swam in a bowl beside them.

"I won't keep anything from you anymore," promised Aunt Cora. She wiped a tear from behind her glasses. "Part of me was afraid to lose you. You're my only family. I was afraid if you found out more about where you come from, you wouldn't want to stay with me anymore." Aunt Cora's lip trembled. "That was selfish, and I'm sorry. I will do everything I can to help you find out where you come from."

"I love you," said Delphi. "I could never leave you behind." The two hugged once again.

Kai felt like they had hugged a million times since they'd gotten to shore. He didn't feel much like hugging, though. He had let the blaster and the crystal egg smash. Now Pineapple Cove was doomed.

Aunt Cora turned to Kai. "Aren't you enjoying the sunset?" she asked.

Kai shook his head. "No, how could I? The whole island is never going to see the sun again. And I am the worst Protector ever. A good Protector would have saved the blaster and the crystal egg."

"Oh, Kai," said Aunt Cora. "You were the perfect example of a Protector today. You made a hard decision and chose to save a helpless animal. And not just any animal. An animal who hasn't made your mission very easy. You showed bravery, kindness, and integrity. If that isn't the best kind of Protector, then I don't know what is."

Kai smiled, but it didn't last. "Maybe, but I still couldn't save the sun."

"If that is true, what am I watching set in the sky?" Cora asked.

Kai jerked his head upward. "But the egg smashed. How is there still sun?"

"I have a feeling that the energy from the egg transferred somewhere safe," Cora said. "You know, that energy once lived in another glass egg on my bookshelf. That is, before Delphi smashed it when she was little. That was when Hobbs and Jasper had to find where it went and deliver it to Turtle Mountain."

Delphi gasped. "I remember that. Well, I remember breaking something glass and round." She flipped her palm up to show a small scar.

"So Pineapple Cove is going to be okay?" Kai asked. Relief washed over him like a big ocean wave. "Where do you think the energy went?"

"I think so," Cora said. "As for where the energy transferred, I'm not sure. It took Hobbs and Jasper years to find it the first time. There were only supposed to be three crystal eggs, but maybe there is another. I'm sure it will turn up eventually."

Kai smiled and looked down at Poseidon. He wasn't sure if he was really meant to be a Protector, but he was glad his home was safe. He let out a big yawn.

The trio stood up on the beach just as Sammy zipped by, chasing a seagull. They all laughed.

A cool breeze brushed past them as they walked to Aunt Cora's house. Out on the water was a large silhouette paddling to shore on a raft. Another silhouette swam beside it.

Kai stopped and squinted at them. He thought it was Hobbs and Jasper, and he was half right. Hobbs and Hermes met up with them on the shore.

"Blue said you wanted me to meet you here," Hermes said to Cora. He flipped his merman tail onto the wet sand and took a seat.

Cora crouched down beside him. She started to say something about Poseidon, but Kai couldn't hear over Captain Hobbs' voice.

"Jasper got away," Hobbs told Delphi and Kai. He tugged the tiny raft to shore. "But I'm sure he will hatch another plan to become King of the Sea. So we will get him next time. Are you guys ready for your next mission?"

"Yes!" Kai and Delphi both cheered

followed by yawns.

Hobbs laughed. "Don't worry, not right now." He led them to his ship, which he had docked beside Aunt Cora's house. It looked like a piece of moldy Swiss cheese with all its holes and green slime. Kai doubted it would float for a minute.

"First, I will need your help to repair these slime cannonball holes," Hobbs explained. "We might need the ship to go get Poseidon's trident. He needs it to turn back into his human form."

Kai was excited at the thought of finally getting to talk to Poseidon. He wanted to ask him why he had really been chosen to be a Protector. Kai yawned once more. But right now, he was most excited about sleep. He sniffed the air. The sweet smell of coconut wafted out of Cora's house.

Okay, and maybe some coco-nutty cookies.

HIDDEN PINEAPPLE ANSWER KEY

There are 16 pineapples hidden throughout the illustrations in this story. Did you spot them all?

CHAPTER 1 = 🍍

CHAPTER 2 = NONE

CHAPTER 3 = 🍍

CHAPTER 4 = 🍍

CHAPTER 5 = 🍍

CHAPTER 6 = 🍍

CHAPTER 7 = 🍍 🍍

CHAPTER 8 = 🍍

CHAPTER 9 = NONE

CHAPTER 10 = 🍍 🍍

CHAPTER 11 = 🍍

CHAPTER 12 = 🍍

CHAPTER 13 = 🍍

CHAPTER 14 = 🍍 🍍

CHAPTER 15 = 🍍

QUESTIONS FOR DISCUSSION

1. What did you enjoy about this book?
2. What are some of the major themes of this story?
3. If you were a fish, what type of fish would you be? Why?
4. What are Kai and Delphi's strengths? What is something you are good at?
5. How did Kai and Delphi work together in the story? When have you worked together with someone?
6. The Legend of Pineapple Cove Book #3 ends with some loose ends. What do you think will happen in the next book in the series?

For more discussion questions, visit thelegendofpineapplecove.com/bundle

THE POWER OF CRYSTALS AND GEMS

Did you know there are many different kinds of crystals and gems that exist in the world? Some people believe each one has a unique power or ability.

A birthstone is a gemstone that represents a person's period of birth, such as the month they were born. Do you know your birthstone and its unique quality?.

JANUARY
garnet
PROTECTION

FEBRUARY
amethyst
WISDOM

MARCH
aquamarine
SERENITY

APRIL
diamond

MAY
emerald

JUNE
moonstone

To learn more about crystals and gems, visit

thelegendofpineapplecove.com/bundle

ADD MORE ITEMS TO MATCH IN THE WATERFALL REFLECTION!

ADD COLOR AND PERSONALITY TO THIS TURTLE MOUNTAIN ELDER!

For more coloring pages, visit:

thelegendofpineapplecove.com/bundle

THE LEGEND OF PINEAPPLE COVE

PROTECTOR'S PLEDGE

By **Marina J. Bowman**

Illustrated by **Nathan Monção**

CONTENTS

1. Werewolves Love Peanut Butter • 339
2. The Missing Trident • 347
3. Scribble Gold • 355
4. Red-Cocooned Creature • 360
5. Ex-Pirate • 365
6. Under Your Nose • 374
7. Mismatched Maps • 380
8. Ralphie • 387
9. Beetle Island • 393
10. Treasure • 400
11. Golden Mop • 406
12. Birds of a Feather • 413
13. Charge! • 420
14. Trapped • 427
15. Just Another Fish in the Sea • 433
16. Friend or Foe • 437
17. Revenge • 442
18. The Distraction • 448
19. Nowhere to Run • 454
20. Poseidon's Protectors • 465

EXTRAS

 Pineapple Answer Key • 471

 More LoPC • 472

About the Author • 481

CHAPTER 1

WEREWOLVES LOVE PEANUT BUTTER

Maya sat in the rusty red wagon with twenty-one jars of peanut butter. The jars clinked and clanked over every bump on the stone path. The four wheels whined with every turn.

Squeak. Squeak. Squeak.

"This would be much easier if I didn't have to pull you too," Kai said to his little sister. He grumbled as he moved the wagon off the path and onto the park's grass.

"Someone has to make sure the peanut butter jars don't break," Maya said. "Hobbs is counting on us."

They weaved around the tall palm trees

and the picnickers scattered on the grass. A soft breeze carried the zingy smell of freshly cut grass and salty seafood sandwiches. Kai's mouth watered.

"If you tell me the story again, I'll walk," Maya said. "How did Captain Hobbs' ship get all slimy and broken?"

"I've told you like a hundred times," Kai said as he rolled his eyes and tried not to smile. He pretended to be tired of telling the story. But really, he loved telling it to anyone that would listen.

"I know," Maya said. "But it is such a cool story!"

He couldn't disagree with that. He didn't know any other ten-year-olds that got to go on such exciting adventures. Well, except Delphi. And he wished he was with her instead of pulling the squeaky wagon through the park. She got to go with their merman friend, Hermes, on an underwater mission. A mission that Kai thought was far more important than finding peanut butter around town.

Kai was sure he didn't get to go because he had made so many mistakes on other missions. He was starting to wonder if he was really meant to be part of Poseidon's Protectors.

"Kai!" Maya whined, snapping Kai away from his thoughts. "Start the story."

"Okay. Okay. The ship had a sail like a big balloon," Kai began. "Me, Delphi, and Captain Hobbs were flying high into the sky to Turtle Mountain. We were on an important mission to save the crystal egg."

"Hey, Sammy the sea lion was there, too!" Maya exclaimed. She crossed her arms over her chest.

"Yes, Sammy was there, too," Kai said. "So we're getting closer when suddenly, we hear 'BANG! BANG!' The mountain was shooting our ship with slime cannons. The ship was almost done for, but Captain Hobbs flew it right next to the mountain. It was close enough for me and Delphi to jump."

Kai stopped by a trio of small birds floating in a bean-shaped pond. He hopped up on a big, smooth rock.

"Slime cannons are hitting the ship. 'BANG! BANG!' It can't take much more. Then, me and Delphi jumped!"

Kai went to jump on the grass, but his sandal slipped the other way.

"Woah!" he cried. He flapped his arms as he leaned back, trying to balance.

SPLASH!

It was no use. He fell backwards into the cool, mucky water. The birds ruffled their orange-and-blue feathers before flying into the sky.

Kai spit out water and sighed. "Then we saved the day, but Jasper the bad guy who stole the crystal egg got away. And Poseidon is still stuck as a fish. The end," he said in one long breath.

Maya laughed as she helped Kai out of the pond. She plucked a blue-and-orange feather from his hair.

"Kai, are you okay?" called a voice nearby. They turned toward their mom sitting on a checkered picnic blanket spread across the grass. Beside her was Kai's dad, wearing his favorite blue fish shorts. Round white plates sat on the blanket as well, along with a tall bundle of flowers displayed in a drinking glass.

"Yeah, I'm fine," Kai answered.

"Are you ready for our picnic?" Kai's dad asked Maya. "Unless you want to swim with

the pond birds first too." He winked at Kai, whose clothes were dripping wet.

Maya laughed and shook her head. "I'm still helping with a mission."

"Ooo, a mission. Watch out for werewolves," Kai's dad joked. "The full moon comes out at eight tonight, and werewolves love peanut butter." He pointed to the wagon piled with jars and howled like a wolf.

Kai laughed. "How do you even know that?"

"Us fishermen always know our moon phases," Kai's dad said.

"No, how do you know werewolves love peanut butter?"

Kai's dad shrugged. "Doesn't everyone love peanut butter? It only seems right that werewolves would too."

"Werewolves?" Maya gulped. "There are going to be werewolves on this mission?"

"Maybe," said Kai. "There might be vampires too."

Maya's lip trembled.

"Kai!" scolded his mom. "Don't scare your sister."

Kai sighed. "Fine. No, there won't be. There is no such thing as werewolves or vampires. But you've already done your job, Maya. You should go."

"Plus, you'll miss out on the cookie salad if you don't stay," Kai's mom said. She pulled out a small glass jar with a silver lid from her picnic basket. It was filled with creamy vanilla pudding and chunks of pineapple and oranges. Right on top was one of Aunt Cora's homemade Coco-Nutty cookies.

"Okay," Maya said as she licked her lips. "I will go with Mom and Dad to keep them safe. You know, just in case. But, Kai, you have to tell me everything! Promise?"

Kai gave his sister a hug. "Promise!"

Maya howled like a mini wolf as Kai pulled the wagon away. Her howl was much squeakier and quieter than their dad's.

Kai laughed and howled back. He pulled the wagon through thick grass and a squishy mud puddle toward the biggest hill in the park. He was starting to feel the park wasn't the best shortcut to get back to Aunt Cora's house.

"Arf! Arf!"

He squinted against the sun and gazed toward the familiar sound. A blubbery gray sea lion was flippering down the hill. Delphi was close behind. Kai met her halfway up. She wiped her wet, purple-streaked hair out of her eyes as she tried to catch her breath.

"I've been looking everywhere for you!" Delphi huffed. "We have a big problem. The rumor is true—Poseidon's trident is missing!"

CHAPTER 2
THE MISSING TRIDENT

Squeak. Squeak. Squeak.

Kai, Delphi, Sammy, and the rusty wagon raced around the corner to the town square.

"What do you mean, the trident is missing?" Kai whispered.

People weaved in and out of the small shops. They circled the fountain with a mermaid spitting water in the middle. A group sat on the edge, snacking on lobster kabobs from Kai's favorite restaurant on the island. His stomach rumbled at the buttery smell.

"The trident wasn't there," Delphi whispered once they were farther away from the crowd. "Hermes and I checked the rock crevice in front of Poseidon's Temple. Right where Poseidon told us to. But we couldn't find it."

"But Poseidon needs his trident. He can't transform back into his human form without it," Kai said.

They whizzed past the antique shop with gold and silver treasures glimmering in the window. It wasn't long before Delphi paused in front of an empty shop with red bricks and a purple door. A crooked 'For Sale' sign hung in the window.

"Why are we stopping at the old ice cream shop?" Kai asked. "It closed when Mrs. Delta retired last month. We should go find Poseidon and see if he can help."

Delphi pushed the door open. "That's exactly what we're doing."

Ding-a-ling.

The silver chimes clinked as the door opened. Cora walked out of a doorway that was covered by a velvety blue curtain. Beside it, a drippy ice cream cone was painted on the back wall. One of the ice cream drips was a clock. Kai wrinkled his nose. He remembered when the shop used to smell like fresh bananas and strawberries. Now it smelled like burnt toast.

He walked around the square, empty room, the floorboards creaking with each step. There were no more photos of ice cream cones and sweet treats on the walls, just nails where they used to hang.

"Is this going to be a Poseidon Protectors' secret clubhouse?" Kai asked, his brown eyes widening.

"No, nothing that exciting," Cora said with a laugh. "I'm thinking about opening a small bake shop here, and Mrs. Delta said I could test the oven today. But it looks like she may have forgotten some ice cream cones in it." Cora frowned as she held up a crumbly, burnt cone.

Sammy flippered up to Cora and snatched it from her hand. He dragged it to a sunny spot on the floor.

CRUNCH! CRUNCH!

Black crumbs sprinkled the old wood floor with every bite.

"I thought you said Poseidon was here."

Kai said. There was no fish tank in sight. In fact, there wasn't much of anything. The only furniture in the room was a round wood table pushed into a corner.

Delphi crinkled her nose. "I thought he would be."

"Oh, he is," Cora said. She plopped down her straw purse on the wood table. It had a pink ribbon tied on the strap and a red button sewn at the top. She undid the button and lifted the straw flap. Underneath was a rectangular fish tank with Poseidon swimming in it. The fish's smart eyes and sharp teeth gleamed as he waved to Kai.

"Woah, that's so cool!" Kai said as he waved back. Sewn inside the flap was the tag that Maya put on all her inventions—a pale pink heart with the initials MCL.

"Maya made this purse for me so I can take Poseidon wherever I go," Cora explained. "So we know he is safe." She rubbed her shoulder. "It was a very smart idea. But we should give him the trident soon, because carrying around a fish tank sure is heavy. Did you and Hermes find it?"

"It wasn't there!" Delphi said. She kneeled beside the fish-tank purse. "Poseidon, are you sure the trident was in your temple?"

Poseidon swam up and down. That meant yes. He swam over to a pen sitting beside a waterproof notepad on the pebbles of his fish tank. The pen had two slots on the side that looked like tiny rubber oven mitts. Poseidon slipped his two front fins into them, and he wiggled his body to draw.

A stream of red ink spluttered from the pen onto the pad. He drew a circle with small dots sprinkled around it, a plus sign, a fork, an equal sign, and a frowning fish.

"He wants to eat a crumbly cookie with a fork!" Kai guessed. Poseidon swam left, then right, which meant no. Kai was wrong.

"Wait, maybe that fork is his trident," Delphi said. Poseidon swam up and down. Delphi was right.

Kai's face flushed red. He felt foolish for

his cookie-and-fork guess.

"Is your trident in a hole?" Kai guessed. Poseidon swam left and right. Nope.

"That last picture is you as a sad fish. Right?" said Cora. Poseidon swam up and down. Yes.

"Okay, so something with a circle and a trident will make Poseidon sad," Delphi said.

"But what is that circle?"

Kai paced the room, and the floorboards creaked under every step. Each one moaned and groaned, but one right in the middle of the room squeaked like a tiny howling wolf. Kai smirked, thinking it sounded like his sister's squeaky wolf howl.

He remembered all the times his dad had taken him and Maya to the beach to look at the full moon. He loved lying on the sand and looking at the stars. Even if the bright, round moon made it a bit harder to see them sometimes.

Kai gasped. "That's it!" He crouched to look at Poseidon. "Is that a full moon?"

Poseidon swam up, then down. It was!

"I think I got it," Delphi said. "If Poseidon doesn't get his trident by the full moon, it will be too late. He will be stuck as a fish forever." Poseidon swam up, then down. Delphi was right.

"Oh no! The full moon is tonight at eight!" Kai cried. He turned to the drip clock on the wall. It was already five. "We only have three hours to find that trident."

CHAPTER 3
SCRIBBLE GOLD

Delphi paced the empty ice cream shop. "So if we don't find the trident in three hours, Poseidon is stuck as a fish forever?" she said.

Kai nodded. His heart banged in his chest like a drum. If Poseidon were stuck as a fish, he might never find out if he was truly chosen to be a Protector. That fish pen and underwater pad that Maya had invented helped, but he was still hard to understand.

"I'm afraid it gets worse," said Cora. "A fish can't be King of the Sea. If he is stuck as a fish, Pineapple Cove will get to vote on who will replace him. And that could be anyone. Including Jasper."

"Oh, no. What if Jasper stole the trident so Poseidon can't transform back?" Delphi asked.

Kai wiped his clammy hands on his shorts. The thought had crossed his mind, too. After all, Jasper did say he wanted Poseidon's title as King of the Sea. He even went so far as to steal the crystal egg to try to make that happen. But something Poseidon had said made Kai doubt it was Jasper.

"The trident couldn't have been stolen," Kai said. "Poseidon said that he put it where no man could get it. So only he could grab it."

Cora exhaled sharply. "I sure hope you're right. We need a plan to find that trident."

The wood floorboard creaked as Delphi plunked down beside Sammy. He was fast asleep in the warm sunspot on the floor. Delphi patted Sammy's blubbery head with her left hand. In her other hand, something flat and round shimmered in the sun.

"What's in your hand?" Kai asked.

"Oh, I forgot about this," Delphi said. "I found this gold coin at the temple, near where the trident was supposed to be. I meant to ask Hermes about it, but then I forgot all about it when we realized the trident was missing." She flipped the shimmery gold coin to Kai.

Kai squinted at it. "The squiggles on it look familiar," he said.

Delphi nodded. "I thought so too, but I don't know where I've seen it before."

Kai squeezed his eyes shut, trying to remember. "Oh! I think I saw them in the pirate tunnel. The one we took under the beach to save Hobbs on our last mission."

Cora took the coin next. "This is pirate scribble gold. It isn't real gold. It's a painted brass coin that they leave behind when they steal something." She scratched off some gold paint with her nail.

"But Poseidon told us it was somewhere no man could get it," Kai reminded Cora.

"Maybe they found a way around it. Pirates are known to be very crafty," Cora said. "I don't know for sure, but there's someone who will. You need to go talk to Captain Hobbs."

Kai, Delphi, and Sammy raced out of the town square and down to the beach. Their sandals flipped and flopped as they sprinted down the shoreline. The sound scared the birds diving for fish nearby. One even dropped its latest catch as it flew away.

Soon they spotted Captain Hobbs' large ship beached in front of Aunt Cora's small, twisty house. Well, if you could call it a ship anymore…

Kai thought it looked more like a pile of scrap wood. A pile that monster-sized termites had snacked on. There were a dozen holes the size of beach balls blown through the ship's whale-sized wooden hull. Then there was the green slime splattered everywhere from the deck to the deflated sails. The slime had once been wet and slippery. Now it was thick and sticky from roasting in the hot sun and smelled oddly sweet.

"Captain Hobbs!" Delphi called. "Hobbs!"

"Aarf! Aarf!" joined Sammy.

"Captain Hobbs!" Kai yelled as he jumped onto the sticky ship. He hopped over the puddles of slime as he looked around the wooden upper deck, but Hobbs was nowhere to be found.

"Maybe he got kidnapped again?" Delphi said from down on the beach. "Um, Kai…" Delphi said in a lower voice. Her eyes widened as she stared over his shoulder. "I think we have company." A tall shadow fell over Kai.

CHAPTER 4

RED-COCOONED CREATURE

Kai whirled toward a towering red creature. It had no arms and two big blue eyes peeking from a red cocoon. It grumbled loudly as it hopped up and down.

"Get back!" Kai shouted. The red-cocooned creature continued to hop in one spot, making a loud thumping noise.

"Yeah, get back!" Delphi yelled. The armless monster hopped higher and grumbled louder.

Delphi grabbed a red sandcastle bucket full of water from the sand.

SPLOOSH!

She threw the water at the creature. It

stumbled backward onto the upper deck and fell to the wood boards with a thump! Its two feet with heavy black boots wiggled in the air. Kai only knew one person who wore heavy boots like that in warm weather.

"Hobbs?" Kai said.

Another muffled sound came from the creature.

Kai twisted and twirled Hobbs until the last of the fabric unwound. It fell to the ship's deck like a red puddle. Hobbs was free.

"It was that sticky goo again!" Hobbs grumbled with a frown on his bearded face. "The ship's sail was stuck in it. I tried to pull it out, but then it ripped, and I fell backward and got tangled in it. I've been stuck like this for almost an hour."

"We have a bigger problem," Kai said. He and Delphi explained the missing trident, the full moon, and the pirate's gold.

"Mother of Pearl!" cried Hobbs. "You need to go see Theodora. She is an ex-pirate who can help you. Ask her about where the pirate

treasure is and tell her that I sent you. You can find her working at the Broken Barrel. Do you two remember where that is?"

Kai and Delphi both nodded. How could they forget? It was a ship that had gotten stuck on a rock out at sea. If that wasn't memorable enough, it was also where they had first met Captain Hobbs.

Delphi looked at the ship full of holes and slime. "But if the ship is broken, how are we going to get there?" she asked.

Kai knew the answer. "The same way we got there when we first went to go meet Hobbs. We can use my dad's sailboat."

"Exactly," Hobbs said. "I'm going to stay here and try to fix the ship before you get back. I've worked with pirates around Pineapple Cove before. They always hide their treasure out at sea, so I have a feeling we will need this ol' gal." He patted the slimy boat. "Did you bring the peanut butter?"

"Oh no! I left the wagon full of jars in the town square! It's in front of the old ice cream shop," Kai said. He felt like he had messed up once again. He wondered if this was why he hadn't been asked to take the official Poseidon's Protectors pledge yet.

"That's okay, I'll go grab them," Hobbs said. "You guys need to go. Now."

Kai, Delphi, and Sammy bolted down to the sailboat. The ocean waves clanked the boat against the side of the dock.

Quickly, the trio hopped in, Delphi untied the boat, and away they went. Next stop: The Broken Barrel.

CHAPTER 5
EX-PIRATE

Kai and Delphi paddled out as fast as they could in the small wooden boat. Sammy lay between them and hung his head over the side, watching the fish. Every once in a while, he would dip his flipper into the water to try to snatch one.

It wasn't long before the shore disappeared. All that was around them was the salty smell of the sea and wavy blue water.

"What was it like underwater with Hermes?" Kai asked.

A big smile spread across Delphi's face. "Amazing! I can't wait to spend more time there after Poseidon gets his trident. I really want to find other Artemis mermaids like me."

Kai swallowed a lump in his throat. "What if we don't get the trident back in time?"

"We can do it!" Delphi said. "We're Poseidon's Protectors."

Kai wished that he felt as confident as she did. The longer he was a Protector, the more he felt like maybe he wasn't cut out to be one. After all, he had made a lot of mistakes on missions.

Kai's paddle splished and sploshed as he dug it into the water. Soon the outline of a ship appeared on the horizon. The Broken Barrel teetered on a rock just in front of them.

They rowed their boat up to the shipwreck. The sound of singing was louder the closer they got.

They anchored their boat on a dock and hopped from barrel to barrel to reach the door. The Broken Barrel was exactly how Kai remembered. It was full of sailors and seafarers singing and eating. The smell of fried fish wafted through the whole pub. Kai was also pretty sure that the same song they had heard last time was playing.

"How will we know which one the ex-pirate is?" Delphi whispered.

Tap. Tap. Tap.

A waitress with a peg leg, an eye patch, and long black hair walked to an empty table. She cleared the dirty plates onto a silver tray.

"That must be her!" Kai said. "Excuse me!" he called across the room. He ran to her side. Delphi and Sammy followed.

"We were told that you can help us. We were wondering what you could tell us about—" Kai leaned in closer and lowered his voice to a whisper. "What you could tell us about the pirate treasure."

The waitress leaned down. "Oh, I know exactly why you are here!" she said with a wink. "Follow me."

Kai's heart fluttered. This was going better than he had imagined.

Tap. Tap. Tap.

The peg-legged waitress led Kai and Delphi to a purple trunk in the corner. She popped open the gem-lined lid. Inside was a rainbow of squishy rubber balls.

"The best treasure the Broken Barrel offers!" the waitress said with a cheery smile.

Sammy grabbed an orange ball in his mouth and flippered away.

At least someone is excited about this treasure, Kai thought.

"Um, thank you, but that's not the type of treasure we meant…" Delphi said.

"We are looking for real treasure," Kai added. "Captain Hobbs sent us."

The waitress shrugged. "This is all I got."

"But as an ex-pirate, you must know where the pirates hide the real treasure," Kai said.

For the first time, the waitress's smile disappeared. "What makes you think I am an 'ex-pirate'?" she growled. Her peg leg tapped the wooden floor loudly.

Kai's cheeks burned red. He didn't know what to say. The waitress adjusted a name tag that read 'Dina.' He had the wrong lady!

"I'm—I'm sorry," he stuttered.

Dina's smile popped back up. "I'm just messing with you," she said. "I get that a lot. But you really shouldn't judge people by how they look." She pointed to the short blonde behind the bar. "I think you're looking for Theodora."

Kai's body felt frozen like a popsicle. He was so embarrassed.

"Thank you!" Delphi said. She turned to Kai after Dina walked away. Her cheeks bulged as she held in a laugh.

Kai groaned. "Oh, be quiet! I was in a rush and didn't read the name tag."

"Maybe I should do the talking," Delphi said. Kai agreed.

"What can I do for you?" Theodora asked as the duo walked up to her. Her lips were bright pink, and she wore a flowy dress with a yellow feathered hem. She was nothing like Kai had imagined a pirate would look.

"Our friend Hobbs said you could help us. We are looking for pirate treasure," Delphi explained.

"Oh yes, Hobbs!" Theodora squealed. "I sure do miss him around here. I still can't get over what that awful 'friend' Jasper did to him. Tsk. Tsk. If it wasn't for Jasper framing him for breaking that portal, he would still be a Protector, you know."

Kai and Delphi glanced at each other. They

had wanted to know more about why Hobbs was fired from Poseidon's Protectors ever since they met him. Kai had so many questions, but he knew they had to stay on track.

Theodora's gaze fell to Kai's trident necklace. "But why am I telling you? I see you two are also Protectors." She looked at the

watch on her wrist and frowned. "Oh dear, I have to go. My shift is over." She turned toward the back door behind the bar.

"Wait!" Kai cried. "We need to know where the pirate treasure is. Hobbs said you would know."

Theodora bit her lip, scraping off some of the thick lipstick. "I can't give you an exact location, but I can tell you this: part of the answer is under your nose. Where the other half is, no one knows."

Kai groaned. He had been hoping it wouldn't be another riddle.

"Are you sure that's all you can tell us?" he asked.

"Positive," Theodora said. "That's all I told the man with the funny mop hair who was in here just before you. But I like you two, so have a Piña Pop on the house." She pushed two glass bottles filled with fizzy liquid toward them. "Good luck."

"Mop hair?" Kai mumbled.

Theodora popped out the door and then

stuck her head back in. "Whoever has a wood sailboat parked on the dock, you've sprung a big leak!" she announced.

Kai's breath caught in the back of his throat. He and Delphi raced outside. Water gushed in through a golf-ball-sized hole at the bottom of their sailboat.

The boat was sinking. Fast.

CHAPTER 6

UNDER YOUR NOSE

"Our boat is leaking!" Delphi cried. *SPLISH! SPLASH! SPLISH! SPLASH!*

Kai and Delphi stood in the boat. They dug like dogs to bail out the water. Slowly but surely, the water level dipped. But every time they almost got it all out, more flooded back in.

"Argh!" yelled Delphi. "Maybe we should just swim."

"That will be too slow. Maybe if we paddle super-duper fast, we can get to shore before it floods."

"I don't think so," Delphi said. "We're pretty good paddlers, but we aren't that fast."

SPLISH! SPLASH! SPLISH! SPLASH!

The duo scooped out more water.

Delphi hopped back onto the dock. "If this boat sinks, it doesn't matter if we solve the riddle. We will never get back to shore in time."

"Then we need to plug that hole!" said Kai.

Sammy flopped into the boat. He tried to put his flippers over the hole, but it kept gushing. Next, Kai tried to stuff his trident necklace in the hole, but the hole was way too wide.

"What's this?" Delphi asked as she bailed water out. She held up something that looked like a long, wiggly worm. But it wasn't a worm—it was spaghetti.

Kai remembered the fake trident made from a broomstick and spaghetti. The one that Jasper had made.

"Jasper was here!" he exclaimed. "I bet you he put a hole in our boat."

Delphi gasped. "I bet you he was also the one who asked Theodora about the treasure before us! He was probably wearing that silly mop wig."

SPLISH! SPLASH! SPLISH! SPLASH!

Kai kneeled on the dock as he scooped more water. He was almost out of breath and not sure how much longer he could keep this up.

Sammy nudged Kai's foot with his new ball.

"Not now!" Kai said. "We have to fix the boat. I'll play fetch with you later."

"Aarf!" cried Sammy. He flipped his ball

into the boat. It floated to the top of the water.

"Wait!" Delphi said. "Try plugging the hole with the ball."

Kai grabbed it. It was super squishy and easy to twist and squeeze. He smooshed it in his palm to make it as small as he could. Then, he jammed it in the hole and slowly lifted his hand. The orange ball stayed in place— it worked! Water was no longer gushing into their boat.

"Hooray!" Kai and Delphi cheered. They gave each other a high five and then gave Sammy a flipper five.

SPLISH! SPLASH! SPLISH! SPLASH!

After bailing the rest of the water out of their boat, they plunked down in it.

"I think Jasper is after the trident," Kai said. "He must know that pirates stole it too. That's why he was asking Theodora where the pirate treasure was."

Delphi gulped. "And if Poseidon doesn't get his trident, then he is stuck as a fish. That means Jasper has a real chance of becoming

King of the Sea."

"Then we need to solve that riddle and get to the trident before Jasper does," Kai said. "Theodora said: 'Part of the answer is under your nose. Where the other half is, no one knows.'"

"Hmm," Delphi said. She crossed her eyes and looked under her nose. "My lips and mouth are under my nose. But I don't think that is it."

"We need to get going," Kai said, picking up a paddle. "We can think on the way."

Delphi continued to fan her face. "I know. But I think I need a drink to cool down first." She eyed the Piña Pop sitting beside her on the wood bench and licked her lips. "And that Piña Pop sure does look good." Kai couldn't disagree with that.

They unscrewed the tops of the glass bottles, and the Piña Pop crackled and fizzled. Kai took a whole mouthful of the bubbly liquid. It tickled his tongue with its fruity, sweet taste. He turned the label toward him. He'd had Piña Pop many times before, but mostly in a glass, so he never got to see the bottle. It was wrapped with a paper label with half a map.

Delphi tipped the bottle into her mouth once more. "Mm, this might be the best flavor I've had," she said.

"I got it!" Kai cried. "The Piña Pop label is right under our nose when we drink it." Kai peeled the label off his bottle to get a better look. "But why is there only half a map?"

"Pirates are very secretive. Aunt Cora told me that some only carry half a map because they feel it's safer. They leave the other half with someone they trust or in a random place…" She gasped. "And I know exactly where that is. It's the same place I've seen that squiggly pirate coin symbol. We need to go back to Aunt Cora's house now!"

CHAPTER 7

MISMATCHED MAPS

The hands on the starfish clock on Aunt Cora's wall said 6:00. They only had two hours to get the trident back to save Poseidon.

They bolted past fish tanks and habitats filled with creatures to get to the stairs. There were glowing frogs, shimmery fish, and ancient turtles. There was a new creature in a silver cage with a tiny pond and grass. It was a small lizard with a leather wing wrapped in a cast. Kai recognized him. It was the same kind of lizard they had seen on Turtle Mountain.

They took the creaky stairs two by two and followed a woven green rug to a dark wood desk. On top of it were rusty metal tea tins that held paintbrushes and a palette with globs of

oil paint. A half-finished canvas of a sailboat sat on an easel nearby.

Above the art desk was what they were looking for—a dozen maps in mismatched frames.

"Which one is it?" Kai asked.

Delphi shrugged. "I don't know. All of the maps with symbols look almost the same."

Kai reached in his pocket and pulled out the Piña Pop label. It dripped with water, and the edges were torn, but the map and pirate symbol were still clear. His gut told him that one of them matched. They just had to find which one.

"This is it!" Delphi exclaimed. She pulled a turquoise frame off the wall. The symbol in the corner matched the one on the coin and the Piña Pop map.

"Good job!" Kai cheered.

Delphi peeled the map out of the frame. It had a drawing of beetles with the alphabet on the back. There was one beetle for each letter.

"Strange. It looks like a code key of some sort," Delphi said.

"Do we need it?" Kai asked.

"I don't think so." Delphi flipped the paper over and pushed it beside the Piña Pop label. The two halves made one complete map. Kai trailed his finger to the island with an X over it.

"This is where the trident should be," Kai said. "It looks like it's just past the archway."

"That's not too far from here! Come on, let's go see if Hobbs' ship is ready."

They ran back outside. The ship had a new red sail raised, but it was still full of slime and holes. Kai circled the ship and found Hobbs and Cora smearing peanut butter on a slime spot. After a few seconds, the peanut-butter-covered slime peeled off the boat like a pancake. A nearby seagull grabbed the slime disk in its beak and flapped away.

"Tell me you two found Theodora and she told you where the treasure is?" Hobbs said. He scratched his nose, leaving a glob of peanut butter behind.

"Well, she didn't tell us exactly, but she gave us a riddle," Delphi said.

"And we figured it out!" Kai added.

Hobbs rolled his eyes. "Pirates and their riddles. I forgot they sometimes carry half-maps with them because they feel it's safer. You know, I hired Theodora and her crew once to help me try to find a pair of ancient earrings for Poseidon. They were able to locate them, but all she would give me was a blasted riddle. Ugh! It still makes my blood boil to this day."

"Why would Poseidon want earrings?" Delphi asked.

Hobbs flipped open his silver pocket watch. "It's a long story that we don't have time for now. Where are we going for the treasure?"

Delphi showed him the map, and the color drained from his face.

"Oh yes, Beetle Island… You know what, you two go ahead," Hobbs said. "Your boat doesn't have room for me anyway." Hobbs glanced at his pocket watch once again. "But you will need this to keep track of time." He dropped the watch into Kai's hand.

Kai ran his thumb over the engraved initials

W.H. Then, with a flick of his wrist, he popped it open. The time read 6:20. They only had an hour and forty minutes left. They didn't have time to argue. Next, Kai turned to Cora.

"I'm going to stay here and watch Poseidon," she said, as if reading his mind.

With that, Kai and Delphi raced back to the sailboat. Kai pushed off shore with his paddle, and they headed toward the archway. Kai's arms ached from paddling so fast by the time they floated past the stone portal.

Delphi pulled out the two map halves. "It isn't too much farther," she said. Sammy hung over the edge of the boat, watching the fish once again.

Suddenly, a long blobby shadow swam under the sailboat. Sammy jumped, spilling Kai's Piña Pop on the deck. He whimpered as he backed away from the edge.

The bubbly Piña Pop spilled out onto the boat's deck. Kai quickly picked up the bottle to try to save what was left.

"Oh no, sorry!" Delphi said. "You can have some of mine."

"That's okay," Kai said. "It could have been worse."

"Um, I think you spoke too soon," Delphi said.

Kai followed her gaze to the squishy ball plugging the hole in their boat. It bubbled and blistered in the Piña Pop puddle.

"Uh oh! It looks like some sort of chemical reaction!" Kai said. He tucked the Piña Pop label into his pocket.

Sammy flippered behind Delphi and covered his eyes.

The ball bubbled and oozed until it began to inflate like a giant soap bubble. First, it was the size of an orange, but before Delphi and Kai knew it, it was taking up most of the boat. The giant bubble was taller than they were, and it wouldn't stop growing.

"Abandon ship! Abandon ship!" Kai yelled. "It's going to blow!"

Splash! Splash! Splash!

Kai, Delphi, and Sammy all dove into the ocean. And just in time.

POP!

CHAPTER 8
RALPHIE

Kai swam to the surface of the water and took a deep breath. The salty seawater stung his eyes. Everything was blurry. Sammy was floating nearby, but there was no Delphi.

"Delphi. Delphi!" he shouted.

GLURP! GLOOP!

Kai watched as the tip of their wooden boat sank into the ocean. Not even the world's best squishy ball could save the boat this time.

"Delphi!" he shouted once more. "DELPHI!"

Something rubbed against Kai's leg underwater. He peered down, hoping to see Delphi, but whatever was down there was much bigger. A dark shadow that was five canoes long swam underneath him. Sammy zipped the other way.

"Good idea!" Kai exclaimed.

Kai kicked his legs as fast as he could. His arms splished and splashed, but no matter how hard he kicked, he wasn't faster than whatever lurked beneath the water.

The shadow swam under him once more. Kai whirled around to see if there was any sign of Delphi, but there was none.

"Delphi!" he shouted once more. He shivered as he trod water. Sammy was swimming away. Kai wanted to swim away too, but there was no way he was leaving without his best friend.

SPLOOSH!

The creature erupted from the water. Waves crashed against Kai, blinding him and filling his mouth with salty seawater. Kai coughed as he wiped the water from his eyes. Everything was a blur once more.

"Delphi?" Kai said as he rubbed his eyes. Delphi sat on a gray whale's back.

"This is Ralphie," Delphi said. "When I

dove off our boat, I saw him underwater. He looked like he needed help, and I was right! He had a barnacle that was too close to his eye. I got it off for him, and now he's good as new."

"You could have told me earlier," Kai spluttered. "I was worried."

"Sorry," Delphi said. "I didn't think I was under there very long."

"It felt like forever to me," Kai mumbled.

Sammy swam back toward Kai and Delphi. He moved very slowly as he kept his eye on Delphi's new friend.

"It's okay, Sammy. He won't bite," Delphi said.

Kai swam up to Ralphie with Sammy to get a better look. Ralphie's skin was slick and spotted with crusty barnacles. Kai ran a hand over a rough patch of barnacles on the whale's side.

"Do these barnacles bother him, too?" Kai asked.

"Nope. Most whales can have a thousand pounds of barnacles without being bothered,"

Delphi answered. "The barnacles act as a suit of armor for the whale, so they don't mind. The barnacles like it too, because they get a free ride and protection from predators."

Kai admired Ralphie's beady eye, which looked like a giant black marble. "I've never

seen a whale this close. He's so big!" Kai said. "This would be so cool if our mission wasn't doomed. There is no way we can make it to the island now. We don't have a boat."

Ralphie made a throaty noise, and Delphi giggled.

She made a whale sound back at him. "Ralphie said he would be happy to help. Hop on!"

Kai pulled himself up onto the whale as Delphi showed Ralphie the map. Then, with one more whale sound, they were off. The cold water splashed against Kai as he rode the whale. He looked behind at his massive whale tail cutting through the water. Sammy was swimming farther behind.

The sun was getting lower in the sky. Kai flipped open the pocket watch. It was six-thirty—they only had an hour and a half. He knew if the trident wasn't on Beetle Island, there was no time for a plan B. Poseidon would be stuck as a fish forever, and Kai would never be a real Protector.

If there was ever a mission where he needed to succeed, Kai knew this was it.

CHAPTER 9
BEETLE ISLAND

The whale swam Kai and Delphi right up to Beetle Island. It was a small sandy patch in the middle of the ocean with a swarm of birds flying overhead. There was a bird of every size and color. Kai spotted red-and-blue parrots, tiny yellow canaries, and chunky black crows.

"It should be called Bird Island," Kai told Delphi.

"What?" Delphi said. "It's hard to hear over the squawking and tweeting." A blue bird swooped down at them. The whale flinched and wiggled until everyone slid off. Then it disappeared into the ocean.

Standing on the shore of the island, they

could see the whole thing. To the left were trees and vine-y jungle plants. On the right was a sandy beach with small rocks. Right in the middle was a giant sandcastle. It was the tallest thing on the whole island. It had a tower on the left side and a wooden drawbridge that crossed the flooded mote.

"That's so cool!" Kai exclaimed. He wondered how big a bucket had been used to make this castle. A "No Trespassing" sign was carved above the entrance.

"I bet that's where they're keeping the trident!" Delphi exclaimed.

Kai agreed. He took a few running steps, but then he stopped. He knew he had to be careful on this mission. It was too important to mess up by rushing. They tiptoed to the sandcastle as they kept an eye out for pirates.

A ladybug landed on Sammy's nose. He went to lick it, but a small bird swooped down and grabbed it.

They crossed the drawbridge and entered the sandcastle. The earthy smell of wet mud filled Kai's nose. Inside there were neither treasures nor pirates. In fact, it was just one empty room with sand and rock walls. Sunlight flooding in through a hole in the ceiling gave the sandy walls an orange glow.

Kai walked to the back wall, the only stone one in the castle. Pictures of beetles were etched on the flat rocks, and a row of skinny pipes stuck out at the bottom.

"It just looks like a big sandcastle," Kai concluded. "I don't see treasure or the trident." He put his eye to the grape-sized opening of one pipe. All he could see was darkness, but something shiny caught the corner of his eye. He bent down and swept sand off a silver plaque on the floor.

Kai read it out loud. "If it is treasure you seek, to the top you must go. But you better move fast. The island name you must know."

He groaned. "Not another riddle." To prove he was a good Protector, he thought he should be doing the stuff he was good at. Like jumping, diving, and fighting off bad guys. Not solving riddles.

TUNK!

The drawbridge sealed the entrance shut. Kai and Delphi ran to re-open it. They pushed and shoved it with all of their might, but it wouldn't budge.

The pipes in the wall creaked and croaked. The sandcastle walls began to shake. Sammy whimpered as he hid behind Delphi's legs.

Psshhhhhh. Psshhhhhh. Psshhhhhh.

They whirled to the strange sound, and Kai's heartbeat quickened. He changed his mind. He wished it were just a riddle.

The pipes in the walls were pouring sand into the room.

"Quick, find a way out!" Delphi cried.

They clawed at the walls, trying to climb them. But the sand crumbled under their weight, revealing smooth concrete walls.

"There goes my idea to dig our way out," Kai said. He moved to the rock wall next. He climbed a couple of rocks up, but the beetle stones he gripped soon slid into the wall. He crashed to the sandy floor as sand poured into the room faster.

"Uh oh!" he cried.

"Wait, I think that's it!" Delphi pulled half of the damp and wrinkly map from her pocket. She flipped it over to the side with all the beetles. "I bet this is a cryptogram."

"A what?" Kai said as he looked down.

The sand was halfway up his shins, and it was getting hard to move.

"A cryptogram. We need to find the answer to the riddle. Then we push the stones to spell the answer out in these beetles." She pointed to the alphabet and matching beetles on the back of the map.

Kai had never heard of a cryptogram before, but he trusted Delphi. "Okay! Let's do this." He dug in the sand, looking for the riddle plaque once more. It was too deep.

Luckily, Delphi remembered. "If it is treasure you seek, up to the top you must go. But you better move fast. The island name you must know."

"Pineapple Cove?" Kai said. "That's an island name."

"Let's try it!"

They matched the beetles to the letters and pushed the stones.

"P," said Delphi as she pushed one stone.

"I found the letter I!" Kai said as he pushed another. The sand sped up, filling the room even faster.

"Oh no, I don't think that's it," Delphi said. The sand was now up to their knees. Delphi pulled Sammy up so he wouldn't get buried.

"Ugh!" cried Kai. "We're going to be stuck here, and Poseidon will never get his trident back on time. No wonder Hobbs didn't want to come to Beetle Island. It's such a silly place."

Kai and Delphi gasped. "Beetle Island!" they both cried.

They matched the beetles to the letters and pushed in the stones. When they reached the last letter, the sand finally stopped.

"Phew, that was close! But how do we get all the way up there now?" Delphi pointed to the opening in the ceiling.

The ground shook like an earthquake.

"I guess we're about to find out," said Kai.

CHAPTER 10

TREASURE

The shaking floor made the grains of sand jump around like popcorn. It felt like a monster was going to burst out from below.

"What's happening?" Delphi cried. Her voice vibrated with the shaking ground.

The sand level started dropping, and a platform with small holes rose under their feet. The sand sifted through the holes like water in a pasta strainer. It wasn't long before it pushed them all the way to the opening at the top of the sandcastle.

The trio was greeted with a burst of fresh air.

Chirp. Squawk. Caw.

Birds flew and chirped overhead once

more. But more importantly, they had found where the treasure was hidden. At the top of the castle, a gold door with etchings of treasure and beetles led into a tower. With one big push, Kai and Delphi opened the door.

CREEEEEAK!

Kai and Delphi looked at each other with wide eyes.

"This must be it!" Kai said.

They stopped just inside the door on a wood platform. Underneath them sparkled chests full of pearls and gold coins spilling onto the floor. Silver statues of mermaids with emerald eyes leaned against the walls, and glass fridges full of Piña Pop were stacked on the other side. The whole room smelled coppery, like a mountain of pennies.

Sand stairs twisted along the wall all the way to the bottom. They followed them for as long as they could, but halfway down, there was a long gap where the stairs had crumbled.

"We are going to have to jump," Kai decided. "I'll go first." With one swift leap, Kai landed on the stairs across the gap and turned around. "Ta-da! Now you and Sammy go— Woah!"

The sand beneath him crumbled. Kai backed up just in time.

"We better move fast," Kai said.

They ran down the twisty stairs, hopping over any gaps. With a small clink, their feet hit the floor, which was covered in treasure. They made it to the bottom and started digging for the trident.

Clink! Clank! Tink!

They sifted through crates of pearls and piles of gold. They found treasure maps and crystals of the sea, along with a collection of figurines with turtle shells. But there was no trident anywhere.

Kai flipped open the pocket watch. It was seven o'clock—they only had an hour left. They had to keep looking. Next, he turned a rusty key in a treasure chest. It popped open to reveal glass balls that shone all the colors of the rainbow. It reminded Kai of the plastic chest in The Broken Barrel.

"Ugh, none of this is right!" Delphi groaned as she dug in a pile of coins. "Where is the trident? We don't have time to dig through this whole room."

"Aarf!" Sammy yelled.

"No, you can't have one of those balls," Delphi said. She turned to look beside her, but her sea lion friend wasn't there.

Kai and Delphi looked around the treasure. There was no Sammy in sight.

"Sammy?" Delphi called. "Sammy!"

"Aarf!" Sammy yelped once more. Kai and Delphi looked up, and there was Sammy, still at the top of the tower. In the big rush, they hadn't noticed that he didn't jump down. Sammy sighed and rested his chin on the ledge.

"I'm so sorry!" Delphi cried. "We will get you down." She grabbed a red flag and unfolded it. She and Kai each grabbed two corners and spread the flag out.

"Jump!" Delphi instructed.

Sammy gave a small whimper. Minutes later, he was still lying on the edge. He would not jump.

"I have an idea!" Kai said. He grabbed an orange ball from the chest. "Jump and you can have this treasure."

Sammy sprang to his feet and dove off the platform. He bounced like jelly as he hit the flag, then climbed off to grab his prize.

THUNK!

A door that blended in with the wall flew open. A man with a pirate's hat stood in front of them. His beard was woven into three braids, two black and one purple.

"Arr, what is going on in here?!" he bellowed. His eyes trailed to Sammy, who was holding the ball in his mouth, and then to Kai and Delphi, who were holding the flag.

They had been caught red-handed.

CHAPTER 11
GOLDEN MOP

Kai, Delphi, and Sammy were led outside of the sandcastle and onto the beach. The pirate with the braided beard stood in front of them. On the brim of his hat under a feather was the name "Remi" stitched in red thread. With him stood a bald man with a shiny head. He was twice as tall as Remi. Beside him was a woman with a scar on her cheek and braided hair that reached her knees.

Chirp. Squawk. Caw.

The swarm of birds continued to chatter above.

"Empty your pockets!" Remi demanded.

They did as instructed. Delphi took out the two map halves and her compass. Kai pulled out Hobbs' pocket watch.

Remi glared at Sammy, whose cheeks bulged. "Empty your mouth, too!" he demanded.

With a sad popping sound, Sammy spit the ball onto the sand.

"Is that everything?" Remi asked.

"Ye—Yes. We promise," Delphi said. Her hands shook.

Chirp. Squawk. Caw.

The pirate collected the items off the ground. "So you came all this way to steal a ball?"

"Aarf!" barked Sammy.

Chirp. Squawk. Caw.

"No, sir," Kai said.

Remi scowled at the sky. "Will you guys give it a rest!" He turned back to Kai. "Speak up. I can't hear you over those loudmouth birds. You know, this was once a peaceful island with no birds. You know what we had? Beetles. Lots and lots of beetles. But then Hobbs had to come and mess that up."

"He sure did!" yelled the tall pirate.

"What did he do?" Kai asked.

"Oh, I will tell you what he did. He hired me and my crew to help him find some earrings. We did, and he got all mad that we would only give him a riddle. So what does he do? He tells the King of the Sky, Zeus, about our secret island full of beetles. Or at least it used to be full of beetles. Next thing we know, the birds are always here, feasting on our bugs."

Chirp. Squawk. Caw.

"It is always so loud! I can hardly think!" Remi roared as he stomped his foot in the sand. He turned back to Kai and Delphi and dropped their belongings in the sand. "That sandcastle you escaped, we used to have it filled with beetles for the riddle. Now we don't have enough beetles thanks to the birds. So we have to use stinkin' sand."

Kai swallowed hard. He was glad it was sand instead of creepy crawly beetles.

Remi sighed. "Well, I guess you two got the riddle right. So you can take one treasure with you. Those are the rules. Is that ball what you choose?"

"Aarf!" cried Sammy. He dove for the ball in the sand and slurped it back into his mouth.

"No!" Delphi and Kai both yelled. Sammy spit the ball out.

"We are here for something you stole from Poseidon," Delphi said.

The pirate rolled his eyes. "You would think the King of the Sea would have good treasure, but he had nothing."

"He did have something! He had a trident, and you stole it!" Kai shouted.

The pirate tapped his fingers on his hairy chin. "Oh! You mean that golden mop?" He and his whole crew began to laugh. "You can have it. It's no treasure. It's no good for nothing."

Sammy's eyes grew wide. "Aarf!" he cried before popping the ball back into his mouth.

"Yes, fine, you can have that treasure," Remi said.

"Wait, you can understand him?" Delphi asked.

"Sure can. My momma was an Artemis

mermaid. She taught me to talk to animals. Some are easier to understand than others. Your sea lion is very easy."

Delphi's mouth fell open. "You're a pirate! Not a mermaid."

"Look, Little Missy," the pirate said. "I am both. Now, do you want that useless mop or not?"

"Yes," Kai answered. They followed the pirates down to their ship, which was hiding behind the tall trees. Remi pulled the trident from the deck. It had a puffy sea sponge speared at the end.

"Like I said, no good for nothing," Remi grumbled. He handed it to Kai, and Kai's heart pitter-pattered. They finally had the trident!

"I'll never understand why a protective charm was around it," Remi continued. "The only one that could grab it was Pasha." He tilted his head toward the girl pirate behind them.

"I guess the trident was where no man could get it, but a woman could," Delphi whispered to Kai.

"What was that?" Remi asked.

"Nothing," Delphi said. "Thank you!" They were getting ready to call Ralphie back when a familiar sound whirled overhead.

Squeak. Whoosh. Whoosh. Squeak.

Kai's breathing got heavier as the sky darkened.

SQUEAK! WHOOSH! WHOOSH! SQUEAK!

An engine-powered blimp appeared above them. "JKS" was scrawled in gold writing on the plump, red balloon.

CHAPTER 12

BIRDS OF A FEATHER

SQUEAK! WHOOSH! WHOOSH! SQUEAK!

Jasper's blimp hovered above Kai, Delphi, and the pirates. Jasper's black bird, Persil, dove toward the trident. He tried to snatch it in his beak, but Kai pulled it away.

"Not this time!" Kai yelled as he hugged the trident to his chest.

"Oh, come on!" grumbled Remi. "You're telling me this bird wants that mop, too? You guys do know it can't even swab a ship deck, right?"

A cackle boomed from the blimp. Jasper's inky black hair blew in the wind as he stuck his head off the side. An evil smile crept upon his face.

"Oh no, you foiled my fake plan. But I bet you won't foil this one!"

Kai clutched the trident. He looked around the sandy shore he stood on. The island was still.

Nothing happened.

Jasper cleared his throat. "I said, I bet you won't foil this one." He leaned over the edge and spotted Persil in a tree. The black bird was making googly eyes at a parrot sitting on a branch. "Persil! This was not part of the plan," Jasper shouted. "Ugh, if only I didn't tell Zeus about this island in the first place, he wouldn't have sent so many birds here."

"What?!" growled Remi. "You're the one who ruined Beetle Island with birds?"

Persil whistled, and a flock of birds gathered overhead. They swooped down at Kai like a swarm of bees. In the tornado of wings and feathers, he dropped the trident. Then, with one swift flick of his wrist, Jasper lassoed the trident and pulled it up to his blimp.

"On second thought, maybe I am glad there are so many birds here." Jasper held the trident over his head. Persil flew up and landed on Jasper's shoulder. "Now, when I have this at the full moon at Poseidon's Temple, I will be King of the Sea. See you!"

SQUEAK! WHOOSH! WHOOSH! SQUEAK!

The blimp flew into the clouds and disappeared.

"I didn't mean to drop the trident!" Kai cried. "I couldn't see it with all the birds."

"It's okay," Delphi said. "We will get it back."

Kai fell to his knees on the rough sand. "We don't have enough time. Even if we get the trident back, we won't make it to Aunt Cora's to give it to Poseidon."

"You can do it with our help!" Remi said. "Get on board our ship. We will take you to the temple."

Kai hesitated. "But why would you help us?"

Remi pointed to the birds swarming above. Thick, white bird poop splashed on his shoulder.

"Any man that did this to our island is also an enemy of ours! Let's go get your trident mop-thingy back!"

Remi led them onboard his pirate ship. It had a yellow steering wheel and a creaky upper deck with a mast right in the middle. On that mast were three layers of sails. Kai was pretty sure the bottom one was a star-patterned bed sheet, but it seemed to do the trick. The pirate ship skipped along the waves toward the temple.

"We still need a way to tell Hobbs and Cora to bring Poseidon," Delphi said.

"Aarf!" said Sammy.

"Are you sure?" Delphi asked. Sammy bobbed his blubbery head up and down. "Sammy says that he will tell them."

"What if they don't understand him?" Kai asked. "We only get one shot at this."

"Does anyone have a pen?" Delphi shouted.

Remi took his hands off the wheel and

plucked a feather from his hat. "Arr, I always come prepared. Use my pen." Delphi pulled the Piña Pop label out of her pocket and scribbled a note.

"There!" Delphi's smile dropped into a frown. "But it's going to smear if it gets wet."

"Hold on, I have an idea! Sammy, can I see your ball?" Kai asked. Sammy dropped his slobbery treasure ball into Kai's hand. Kai wiped the ball off on his shirt and twisted the top. The ball popped open, and a gem fell into his hand.

"Woah, how did you know it opened?" Delphi asked.

"I noticed one open in the treasure chest," Kai said. He held the gem up to the light. It sparkled purple and blue. "I don't know what this is." He dropped the gem into his pocket. "But I know the note will fit in here and stay dry. The gem was slobber-free, so I think the note will be safe." They tucked the note into the ball and gave it back to Sammy. Delphi gave him a pat before he jumped overboard.

"Good luck!" she said.

Moments later, their ship arrived at the temple. The pocket watch said 7:40. They only had twenty minutes to find the trident and save Poseidon from being stuck as a fish forever.

CHAPTER 13

CHARGE!

The red balloon on Jasper's parked blimp peeked out over the stone roof of Poseidon's temple. The temple felt much different than when they were there before. The entrance now glowed purple, and it was eerily quiet with no wind or echoes floating out like the first time. But that quiet didn't last long.

The pirates jumped off the ship with their swords in hand.

"Charge!" they all yelled as they stormed the temple. They didn't even reach the door before they got stuck. Their boots were trapped in a puddle of slime. It looked just like the green goop on Hobbs' ship—and it was just as sticky.

"What is this?" Remi growled. "I can't

move."

"Me neither!" said another pirate.

Kai and Delphi carefully crept to the pirates. They tried tugging them and pushing them, but the slime was too strong.

Kai eyed Remi's leather satchel. "Do you have any peanut butter in there?"

"Hey, Buckaroo, is now really the time to be thinking about your stomach?" Remi asked.

"No, it can unstick you from the slime."

"Oh, well, there's no peanut butter. Just some Piña Pop." Remi pulled out a glass bottle.

"That could work!" Kai said.

Kai opened it and started tipping it toward the ground.

"What if it explodes like last time?" Delphi asked.

"Explodes!?" exclaimed Remi. He snatched the bottle back and took a swig. "If you are wasting Piña Pop, you better not be exploding me and my crew. You know what? I have a better idea." Remi slipped off his boots.

Kai and Delphi almost passed out from the

smell. It was a mix of rotten fish and toe jam.

"There!" Remi said before taking another drink of Piña Pop. "Problem solved! Now we have a no-good scallywag to find."

"Oh, are you looking for us!"

Theodora stepped forward with a parrot on her shoulder. With her were two other women. One had a shiny sequined bird on her shirt. The other had an armful of bird tattoos.

"What are you doing here?" Remi snarled.

Theodora shrugged. "Jasper made me an offer I couldn't refuse. After he couldn't figure out the riddle, he hired me to follow these two Protectors. Once they found the treasure, I was to tell him where they were."

"Why wouldn't you just tell him where the treasure was?" Kai asked. "You knew where it was!"

"It's against the pirate code!" Remi said. "And I bet you she was offered something shiny for her services."

"Bingo!" said Theodora. "He offered me a chest of Poseidon's gold."

Remi laughed. "We were at this temple weeks ago. There is no treasure here. Just some golden mop."

"You fool! That is the all-powerful trident that can harness the power of the sea." Theodora drew her sword. "But maybe today isn't about gold or treasure. Let's settle our dispute once and for all, Remi." With a cry that echoed over the temple, she ran at Remi with her sword. The other pirates followed.

Clink. Clank. Clunk.

Swords were clanking together left and right. Kai wanted to watch more, but he knew they had to go. He and Delphi tiptoed to the entrance of the temple.

Statues of people with tridents still lined the walls. But the orbs hanging from stringy seaweed no longer shone blue. They had a thin layer of red paint that gave them a purple glow. They reached the glittering bronze doorway, but there were no blue guards this time. The doors were cracked open.

"Where did the guards go?" Kai whispered

to Delphi.

"They left to go look for the trident when we saw it was missing," Delphi said.

They carefully pushed the door wider and poked their heads in. No one was there. There was no sign of Jasper or Persil—but there was the trident. It sat on the podium where the Storm

Blaster had once been. It was surrounded by water and Finley fish with razor-sharp teeth.

"Look!" Kai exclaimed. He eyed the rope hanging from the ceiling from the last time he had been here. "Don't worry, I've got it." He ran full-speed at the hanging rope, grasped it with both hands, and swung over the Finleys. The fish leaped out of the water, chattering their teeth.

Kai landed on the platform and went to lift the trident, but it was stuck in slime. And so was he. He twisted and wiggled, but the slime was too sticky. It oozed between his toes and sandals. It was like a sticky snake slithering around his feet.

"It's a trap!" Kai yelled, but it was too late. Jasper snuck behind Delphi and dumped a bucket of slime by her feet, trapping her too.

"Oh, this was almost too easy!" Jasper chirped. "It turns out being a bad guy is much better when you think out your plans. So thank you for that advice." He skipped over to the other side of the room and pulled the real trident out from the corner.

Kai's mouth fell open. He looked down at the trident by his feet. It was the costume one—the broomstick with spaghetti taped to it. Spaghetti that now had green moldy spots.

They were tricked and trapped with no trident. If they couldn't get themselves out of this, Poseidon was doomed and Jasper would be the new King of the Sea. And Kai felt like it was all his fault.

CHAPTER 14
TRAPPED

"You're not going to get away with this!" Delphi screamed. She tried to lift her foot from the slime, but it snapped back down like it was tied to a rubber band.

Jasper cackled. "And why not? I planned it all so well this time. I didn't rush into anything." He hit the end of the trident on the ground. "I even have an audience for when I become King of the Sea."

"You still need to win the election for that!" Kai spat. "And you aren't very likable."

Jasper waggled his finger. "Oh no, you have it all wrong. Whoever has the trident in the temple at the full moon becomes King of the Sea. Poseidon has been in charge for hundreds of years, but that ends tonight. Since I have the trident, there is no need for an election."

Kai's throat got tighter. He didn't like the sound of that. He peered at his pocket watch and saw it was 7:55. They only had five minutes.

A crinkling sound filled the temple. Jasper unwrapped a sandwich, and a very familiar sweet and salty smell filled Kai's nose. Peanut butter!

"Wow, that sure looks good," Kai said. "It's been a busy day, and I would love a snack."

"Kai, we have bigger problems!" Delphi hissed.

Jasper glanced at Kai. "I'm a villain, not your personal cook. This is my sandwich."

"But Jasper, you have outsmarted us. We give up," Kai said through clenched teeth.

"No, we don't!" exclaimed Delphi.

Kai turned to Delphi and winked. "Yes, we do. So the least Jasper could do is give me a snack to watch him become the new King of the Sea."

Jasper rolled his eyes. "Fine. Once I am

king, I am sure I will be rich and won't have to eat peanut butter sandwiches." He wrapped the sandwich back up and tossed it to Kai.

"Is that why you want to be King of the Sea?" Delphi asked.

"No," Jasper answered. "I couldn't care less about that. I just want to be liked and respected. Is that so much to ask?"

"Yes, it is," Kai mumbled.

"What?" Jasper asked.

"I said, I think I hear Hobbs outside!" Kai yelled.

"Hobbs?!" Jasper exclaimed. "Yes, he needs to see this, too." He placed the trident back in the corner and bolted outside.

"Why would you say that so loud?" Delphi asked. "Hobbs could have saved us."

"I didn't really hear Hobbs, but I have a plan."

Kai held up the sandwich. "This peanut butter can loosen the slime. Then we can grab the trident."

"That's genius!" Delphi said.

Kai held the sandwich in his hand and froze. "I think you should free yourself and get the trident," he told Delphi. "I've been making a lot of mistakes and don't want to ruin this."

Delphi shook her head. "No way. We wouldn't be here without you. This is your plan, and it's a great one. You can do it!"

Kai was still unsure, but he didn't have time to argue. He unwrapped the sandwich and smeared the peanut butter on the slime. Soon his left foot slid out and then the right. He was free, and so was the spaghetti trident. He hopped down with the moldy spaghetti stick and swapped it with the real trident.

He held the trident in his hand. The metal felt heavy and cold. He looked at the time: only three minutes left. He wondered what would happen if he just held onto it for three more minutes. He would become King of the Sea. Everyone would respect him, and he would never have to worry about feeling like a real Protector…

…But then again, there would be no such thing as Poseidon's Protectors. And he loved being a Protector. Plus, what would happen to Poseidon? He would just be stuck as a fish forever? That didn't seem fair. Footsteps clipped and clopped by the door, snapping Kai away from his thoughts. He made it back atop the podium just in time.

"Aunt Cora!" Delphi cried. Cora entered the temple with Hobbs and Sammy behind her. And on Cora's shoulder was the straw bag with the pink bow. Kai knew Poseidon must be inside. A tall shadow fell on the floor behind Hobbs and crept closer. Jasper appeared, holding another bucket of slime.

"Watch out!" Kai yelled, but it was too late. The slime splattered onto the floor. They were now all trapped.

CHAPTER 15

JUST ANOTHER FISH IN THE SEA

Jasper's laughter echoed through the temple.

"I love it," he said. "Pirates fighting outside and a whole audience to watch me become King of the Sea. And that includes my old bestie, Hobbs." A sly smile stretched across Jasper's face. "Let's see who is more likable after this!"

Hobbs groaned. "Oh, come on! More slime? I just finished getting a ton of this off my ship. I was mad when you framed me for breaking that portal. You got me banned from Poseidon's Protectors and ruined my life! But you know what? I think this is worse! I am so sick of slime. I wish those turtle people never taught you how to make it."

Jasper circled Cora and Hobbs. "I see you didn't bring Poseidon." Cora shifted the bag on her arm, and it made a sloshing sound. "Or did you?" He yanked the purse off of Cora's shoulder. He opened the flap and glared at Poseidon. "Well, hello, little fishy!"

He danced across the temple with the purse over his head. "Oh, could this day get any better?" He looked at his watch. "Thirty seconds to go." He dumped Poseidon in with the other Finleys. "Just another fish in the sea now." Next, he grabbed the fake trident.

Kai held his breath. Luckily, Jasper was too busy pretending the trident was a microphone to notice it was fake.

Jasper started counting down in song. "Ten, nine, eight—"

Kai crouched down and gently plopped the trident into the Finley water. He sure hoped Poseidon found it and not some other fish.

"Three, two, one! I am King of the Sea!"

Jasper yelled. Some of the moldy spaghetti swung into his mouth. He spat it out with a cough and opened his eyes. "Being King of the Sea doesn't taste great. Blah." He looked at his hands. "And I don't feel any different."

"Oh, but I do!" boomed a deep voice. Poseidon stood on the edge of the pool of Finleys with the trident in his hand. He was a

large man with flowing blue hair and the mark of a trident on his chest.

"What!?" Jasper gasped. He gave the trident a good look. Some of the spaghetti slipped onto the floor. "Noo! It can't be!"

Poseidon's legs wobbled as he stepped toward a wide-eyed Jasper. He took another step forward. His ankle turned to the side, and he crashed to the stone floor. The trident flew out of his hand—right to Jasper's feet.

Jasper picked up the trident and bolted out the temple door.

Kai pulled Poseidon by the hand, but his legs just wobbled like jelly.

"Leave me and get that trident back!" Poseidon cried.

Kai looked around the dimly lit temple at Cora, Hobbs, Sammy, and Delphi. All of their feet were glued to the stone floor with globs of sticky slime.

Poseidon looked Kai in the eyes. "You're the only one who can save the trident and Pineapple Cove now."

CHAPTER 16
FRIEND OR FOE

Kai ran out the temple doors. The full moon lit up the island, giving everything from the sand to the anchored boats a creepy glow. There was Remi's ship, Theodora's, and Hobbs'. Hobbs' ship looked by far the roughest, with holes patched with wood and slime bits still sprinkled everywhere.

Kai stopped to listen for footsteps, but all he could hear was the sound of pirate swords clinking and clanging on the shore. There was no sign of Jasper, but Kai knew he couldn't be far. His red blimp was still parked behind the temple.

Kai raced to the blimp. His heart felt like it was beating a million miles per minute. What if he made a mistake and Jasper got away with the trident? He wished the Storm Blaster hadn't broken. He always felt like a true Protector holding it.

BOING!

Thoughts of the storm blaster were bounced right out of Kai's head. As he rounded the temple's back corner, he slammed into a slimy, rubbery wall. It knocked him on his back into the rough sand.

He sat up and looked at what he had hit. It wasn't some sort of slime wall at all. It was a creature that looked like a glob of jiggly green jelly. Except he had arms and two stalks with bobbly eyes poking out from his head.

"Bob?" Kai said. It was the same creature that had once kidnapped his mom and Maya.

The green, globby creature gave a wave that made his whole body jiggle.

"Watch out!" yelled a male voice from behind Bob. Kai squinted through Bob's jelly body. Two blurry mermaid tails sparkled in the moonlight. Hermes the merman and Amphi the

Mermaid Queen were tied back-to-back.

"Behind you!" cried Amphi. But it was too late. A flurry of orange hair flashed as a girl jumped down from a nearby tree. She had a green turtle shell on her back and was holding a wood fishing rod strung with seaweed that had a lasso tied at the end. Kai rolled on the sand and sprang to his feet as she cast her line. She missed.

Squeak. Whoosh. Whoosh. Squeak.

The sounds of the blimp's motor echoed through the heavy, warm air.

"Willow! What are you doing?" Kai yelled at the girl with the fishing rod. He had met the turtle girl on his last adventure to Turtle Mountain. She had been more than happy to help them then, but now she was on Jasper's side?

She drew the fishing rod back and cast at Kai once again. Kai ducked and bolted toward the blimp. He couldn't let Jasper get away.

SQUEAK! WHOOSH! WHOOSH! SQUEAK!

The blimp's motor started running faster. Kai was only a few steps away from the blimp. He was ready to jump, grab hold of it, and climb on board to get the trident back. But it didn't take off as he expected. The motor slowed down before Kai got there. He stopped and stared at the blimp, wondering if it had broken.

Jasper poked his head over the side of the blimp. He held the shiny trident in his hand and had a scowl on his face. "What happened?"

Kai felt a slimy strip of seaweed get lassoed around him. He was trapped, just like everyone else.

CHAPTER 17
REVENGE

Bob the Blob carried Kai over his shoulder and plunked him down with Hermes and Amphi. Kai tried to wiggle free, but the tight seaweed wouldn't budge.

A weird, high-pitched noise echoed from the temple.

Jasper circled his blimp with the trident in hand. "Oh, come on!" He ran his hand over the propeller, which was gummed up with slime.

"Kai! What did you do?" Jasper bellowed. "I will not have a blasted kid ruin my plan once again!"

Kai wiggled against the seaweed. "Nothing. Now let me go! I wasn't even near your propeller."

Jasper let out a frustrated scream. "Fine, you want to gum up my sky ship. I can play that game."

"Jasper, why don't we just take one of the sea ships to get out of here?" Willow asked.

"No!" Jasper said. "Not without my revenge. Now fetch me my slime ingredients." Jasper leaned the trident against the side of the blimp and grabbed an uninflated ducky pool from his blimp. He popped open the air valve and began to blow.

"What is he doing?" Amphi whispered.

Kai groaned. "Probably creating another whirlpool to suck us into." He looked for something sturdy to grab, but there was only the smooth corner of the stone temple behind his back. He gulped.

Jasper's face was as red as a tomato by the time the pool was inflated. It was indeed the same ducky pool from Jasper's hideout, but now it had red patches to plug some holes. Bob and Willow each plunked a metal bucket beside it.

"I can't believe Bob is behind this again," Kai complained.

"That's because he is under a spell," Hermes said.

"We thought he was acting weird, so we followed him. Right as we swam up to shore, that turtle girl tied us up," Amphi added.

"She must be under a spell too!" Kai said. "Willow was too afraid of heights to climb a tree when I met her. But she seemed to have no problem this time."

Amphi groaned in pain. Her tail wasn't as shiny as usual. The scales were turning a brassy color and shriveling. Hermes' tail looked the same.

"Are you okay?" Kai asked.

"For now," Amphi said. "But if we don't get to water soon, we won't be." She groaned again.

Kai struggled against the seaweed, but it was no use. He felt nothing like a real Protector. Tears welled in his eyes. Because of his mistake, his friends were hurting. He shouldn't have allowed himself to get trapped. Again.

He watched as Jasper dumped a bucket of blue ooze into the pool. Then he reached into the other bucket and pulled out a jar of honey. He dumped jar after jar of the sweet yellow goo into the pool. He swirled it around with a stick, making green slime.

"Perfect!" Jasper clucked. "Soon you can feel exactly how my poor sky ship does."

A bead of sweat dripped down Kai's face. He didn't like the sound of that.

"Psst. Psst!" whispered a voice. Poseidon was lying belly-down on the sand behind him.

"There is going to be a distraction. When that happens, I need you to—" Poseidon hiccupped. "I need you to—" Poseidon hiccupped again, but this time a water bubble floated out of his mouth. He opened his mouth to talk, but more bubbles floated out.

Poseidon sighed. Then he dragged his finger through the sand beside Kai. He drew a stick man holding what looked to be the Storm Blaster.

"The Storm Blaster broke," Kai said. "I don't have it to use."

Poseidon continued to draw. He made an equal sign and then another stickman. Except this stick man was holding a giant fork. Kai knew that was the trident.

"But I don't know how to use the trident," Kai said.

Before Poseidon could draw anything else, Delphi ran past them.

"Hey, Jasper, you really should get better at trapping people!" she taunted.

Kai felt Poseidon untie his hands. He quickly freed his feet himself.

This must be the distraction. Now he just had to reach the trident.

CHAPTER 18

THE DISTRACTION

"**W**hat!? How did you escape the slime?" Jasper roared.

"We've been chasing that trident all day. I think you underestimate how hungry a sea lion can get." She turned to the empty jars of honey surrounding the ducky pool. "And Sammy loves honey."

"Get her!" Jasper cried.

Delphi dipped and rolled to avoid Bob's gloopy grasp. And she hopped and dived to outrun the seaweed rope. But she couldn't escape the long, snake-like tentacle that scooped her up. The giant octopus scuttled closer to the blimp, squeezing Delphi in its tentacle.

Jasper's mouth dropped open before turning

into a smile. "Oh yes, you!" he said. "I don't remember putting you under another spell, but this will do nicely."

"You won't get away this time!" Delphi yelled before the octopus covered her mouth.

Jasper cackled. "Oh, I think I will. I planned this perfectly. I even had a Plan B. I put all of these creatures under a spell in case you annoying kids ruined my trident plan. Now all I have to do is keep the trident until the next full moon and I can be King of the Sea!"

Jasper turned to his pool of slime. "But not before I slime you all, like you did my ship." He dipped the metal bucket into the pool and filled it with goo. Then, he turned to Kai. But Kai wasn't beside Amphi and Hermes anymore.

Jasper gasped. "Where is he?" He turned to a shaking bush and walked slowly toward it.

"SQUAWK!" A blue bird flapped out.

"Bob! Willow! Find that little brat," Jasper bellowed. There was no answer. "Where did you guys go?" Next, he called out for his bird sidekick. "Persil? A little help would be great."

But no bird arrived. "Argh. It seems the only one doing their job is that octopus. And I don't even remember putting a spell on him this time."

Muffled yelling came from the direction of the octopus. Bob and Willow were wrapped up in two of its tentacles.

Delphi stood on the sand with her arms crossed. "That's because he isn't under a spell."

"Are you looking for me?" Kai asked. He held the trident by the blimp with shaky hands.

Jasper whirled around. "Give that back!" he yelled.

"Now, Kai!" Poseidon yelled.

"From the oceans cold and warm, I summon Poseidon's storm," Kai said in a small voice. He pointed the trident at Jasper, but only a few drops of water sputtered out. "Um, hello," Kai said, shaking the trident. "It's not working!"

Jasper cackled. "Guess it doesn't work for everyone. You should have saved those drops of water for your poor friends over there." He pointed to Hermes and Amphi lying on the beach. They were passed out, and their tails were browner and more shriveled than ever.

Kai felt bravery bubble in his chest. He clutched the trident tighter. "From the oceans cold and warm, I summon Poseidon's storm!" he cried. Streams of water shot out of the end of the trident spikes like rockets. They melded into one big powerful stream and blasted Jasper

back into the pool of slime.

The powerful stream continued to jet out of the trident. Kai turned it toward where Poseidon was hiding. "How do I turn this off!" he yelled, but Poseidon was gone. "Unsummon the storm! Unsummon!" But the water kept jetting out.

Poseidon's large hands grasped the trident with Kai.

"Turn it toward the sky!" Poseidon commanded. Together they pointed the trident up. The streams of water plopping down made it feel like they were in a rainstorm.

"Now tap it three times on the ground."

Tap! Tap! Tap!

The water stopped. Kai and Poseidon hurried toward Amphi and Hermes. Their tails were less brown from the trident's water, and they were awake. But it looked like they were going to be sick.

"Quick, get them to the water!" Poseidon said. Before he could reach them, he crashed to the sand. "Argh! These darn side effects from being a fish too long. You'll have to do it without me."

Delphi and Kai tried to pull Amphi first, but she was too heavy.

"We can help!" came a small voice. But before Willow and Bob could help, the octopus grabbed both mermaids.

"Wait! Stop!" Kai cried. But the octopus didn't listen. He clasped both mer people with his tentacles and scuttled toward the shore.

CHAPTER 19

NOWHERE TO RUN

The octopus gently placed Amphi and Hermes in the water, and Kai exhaled in relief. The color on their tails quickly came back. And their scales shimmered as the full moon slunk out from behind a cloud.

Remi and the other pirates finally stopped their sword fight to see what all the commotion was about.

"Arr, you all okay?" he asked.

"We are now," Hermes said. "Thanks to Poseidon's Protectors."

"That means we did it!" Delphi cried. She ran up to Kai and gave him a high five. Suddenly, a large tentacle slithered toward them.

"GURGLE! GLORB!" grumbled the

octopus. Kai backed away, almost tripping over a branch sticking out of the sand.

"It's okay, he just wants a high five, too!" Delphi said with a giggle.

Kai cautiously high-fived a suction cup the size of a soccer ball under the octopus' tentacle.

"Isn't this the same octopus that tried to destroy Pineapple Cove?" he asked.

"Yup, it sure is," Delphi answered. "While Sammy ate away at the slime to free me, I started thinking about what Remi had said. You know, about Artemis mermaids talking to animals. I knew we needed help, so I tried calling out in whale. Kind of like how I talked to Ralphie."

"Oh, that's what that weird sound inside the temple was!" Kai crinkled his face. "But you know this is an octopus."

Delphi giggled. "Well, maybe I spoke octopus instead. I really don't understand how this all works yet."

"I can help you with your animal speak, if you'd like," Remi offered.

Delphi's face lit up. "You can?"

"Anything for a fellow Artemis mermaid."

A squidging sound came from beside the temple. Jasper was making a run for it. With the inflatable ducky pool stuck to his back like a turtle shell, he made a hunched-over dash for Remi's ship.

"Oh no you don't!" Remi said. Jasper pivoted and turned back toward the temple. He knocked Cora and Hobbs into the sand just as they exited.

"Follow him!" Poseidon commanded.

Once inside, Jasper waded through the Finley-infested water.

"Ow! Ouch!" he cried as the fish clamped to his pants with their sharp teeth.

POP!

The ducky pool popped as one Finley bit into it.

Jasper clumsily climbed on the podium where the Storm Blaster had once stood. He started to breathe heavily as he realized he was surrounded.

Kai, Delphi, Sammy, Hobbs, Cora, Willow, Bob, Remi, Theodora, and all the other pirates stood around him in a circle. There was nowhere to run.

Poseidon hobbled in using his trident as a cane to support his shaky legs. Once in front of the podium, he pointed the trident at Jasper.

"Wait! I didn't mean any harm. I just wanted to be the one who was liked for once," Jasper said to Poseidon. "You always liked Hobbs better than me, until I framed him for breaking the portal. Then everyone loves you, the King of the Sea, so I thought they would like me too if I had your power."

Poseidon's face turned red with anger. "Well, Jasper. Maybe we should have a chat about how to be more likeable. For starters, you might want to stop betraying your friends. But for now…" He aimed the trident at Jasper once more. "Stuck as a fish you will be until I say you are free!" he chanted. With a puff of smoke, Jasper turned into a Finley sitting in a fish tank. And floating on top was a little rubber duck.

Kai had so many questions, but all he could do was stare at Poseidon. They did it. They had saved Poseidon and caught Jasper.

"What are you going to do with him?" Cora asked. Poseidon squinted at the fish in the glass bowl on the podium.

"Hmm, I'm not sure yet," Poseidon answered. "I will turn him back eventually. Once I find a fitting punishment."

He turned and shook Kai and Delphi's hands. "Thank you! I knew you two could do it. Blue was tasked to pick my Protectors to get me out of this mess," he explained. "When you saved him from that fishing net, he knew you were a good choice." He gave Kai a big smile. "I couldn't have picked a better Protector myself."

Kai shook his head. "But I made so many mistakes. I got caught by Jasper not once, but twice today!"

Poseidon smiled. "You did, but that's part of what made our last plan work. Because of you, Delphi was able to sneak around the other side of the temple and slime the blimp propeller. Jasper was too distracted watching Bob and Willow try to capture you to notice. And not everyone could have used that trident, you know. It is much more powerful than the Storm Blaster, so it is harder to control. But you did great!"

Kai smiled. He had been so busy thinking about all his mistakes that he forgot to remember all the ways he had helped.

"I couldn't have done this without you or Delphi. In fact, I would love for both you and Delphi to take the official Poseidon's Protector Pledge."

"Okay!" Kai and Delphi exclaimed with a little hop.

It felt like a million butterflies were flying in Kai's stomach as he thought about taking the pledge. He was a real Protector. Poseidon knew it, but most importantly, he felt it. Even though he made mistakes, he was still able to help save the day.

"First, maybe we grab some food," said Poseidon. He rubbed his gurgling stomach. "I can't wait to eat something besides fish food! That stuff always leaves you starving."

"I think I know just the place for food!" Cora said. "I think we are all starving."

"Arf!" Sammy barked. He was rolled over, his round belly full of honey slime pointing toward the ceiling.

Delphi laughed. "Well, maybe not everyone."

The group sailed back to Cora's house to enjoy a shrimp stir fry and fresh Coco-nutty cookies. The kitchen was filled with laughter and friendly little squabbles. Kai snatched another crunchy cookie from a plate on the counter as Poseidon asked questions about the pirate duel.

"Did you pirates not think to help when you heard all the commotion?" he asked.

Remi shrugged. "We had important things to duel about."

"Like what?" Kai asked.

"We were settling an argument once and for all," Theodora said. "Remi says birds are good for nothing. I think they're wonderful."

"That's what you were fighting about?!" Delphi exclaimed.

Remi and Theodora both nodded as they glared at each other.

Poseidon sighed and then laughed. Kai looked at Persil sitting with Theodora's parrot on the windowsill. They rubbed their faces against each other. Kai was wondering where Jasper's sidekick had gone. It looked like Persil had skipped the battle this time to make a new friend.

"What do you think of them now?" Cora asked.

Remi shrugged. "They ain't so bad. And speaking of birds, I'm sorry I thought you sent all them birds to our island, Hobbs." He shoved another forkful of shrimp into his mouth. "It turns out it was Jasper." He squinted at the fish in the bowl on the seashell counter.

"Thank you," Hobbs said. "I really thought

I did it, though! I didn't tell Zeus about Beetle Island, but one day I was whistling and one bird showed up. And then another. And another! I thought I was such a good whistler that I attracted all the birds."

Everyone laughed, including Hobbs.

Persil gently pecked at the parrot's colorful feathers with his dark beak.

"What's going to happen to Persil?" Willow asked.

"I don't know," Poseidon said. "I don't think this is his fault."

"I can watch him!" Theodora offered. "I think he really likes my parrot."

Poseidon agreed. He shoved the last of his cookie into his mouth and stood. "I have to go," he said. "But I will see you all again soon."

Kai wanted to ask him about taking the pledge, but he was already gone.

The rest of the night was filled with stories and snacks. Hobbs walked Kai home a little before midnight. The light from the moon spilled over the streets, and a cool breeze swept through the air.

"You did good," Hobbs said just as they turned on Kai's street. A fluffy gray cat scampered across the road and dove into a bush with pink flowers.

Kai yawned and then smiled. "You mean, *we* did good!"

CHAPTER 20
POSEIDON'S PROTECTORS

Knock. Knock. Knock.

"Kai, are you in there?" Maya asked from the other side of the bedroom door.

Kai peeked out from under his sailboat sheets. He looked at the window and squinted at the sun pouring in. He had been dreaming about when they captured Jasper and saved Poseidon a week ago. It still brought a smile to his face.

Knock. Knock. Knock.

"Kai?" Maya cracked open the door and saw Kai stretching. She placed her hands on her hips. "It's rude not to answer the door!"

Kai yawned. "Sorry, I was—" But before

Kai could finish, he saw what his sister was holding. It was an envelope, but not just any envelope—it was a blue one with Poseidon's official aqua seal! He lunged across the room and snatched the letter.

"Hey!" Maya cried.

Kai ripped the letter open. He tried to start reading, but Maya kept talking.

"Can you come see what I made?" Maya asked. "This invention is super good! It is going to be able to teleport people... well, at least I hope."

Kai quickly agreed as he kept his eyes glued to the letter.

A big smile spread across Maya's face. "Okay! I just need an hour to set up." She bolted out of the room, and finally, Kai was left in silence.

Kai sat on the edge of the bed. His heart pitter-pattered with excitement as he read the letter. He couldn't believe it.

Dear Kai,

Thank you for all your work protecting the

island! This letter is to officially invite you to take the Protector Pledge. Please meet me at Aunt Cora's house at 10 AM on Saturday the 16th.

See you soon,
Poseidon

"That's today!" Kai exclaimed. He jumped up from the bed and raced out the front door. It was finally happening.

Kai sprinted down to Aunt Cora's topsy-turvy three-story house. He had never been so excited to skip down Aunt Cora's seashell walkway.

Knock. Knock. Knock.

Aunt Cora opened the door. "Kai, don't you just have the best timing!" she said. "And what a fun outfit." Kai looked down and gasped. In all his excitement, he had forgotten to change out of his pirate pajamas! He was speechless. Aunt Cora winked. "It's okay, we can make it a pajama party. Come on in!"

The sweet smell of Coco-Nutty cookies wafted through the door. Kai was led to the kitchen, where he found Delphi, Captain Hobbs, and Poseidon all snacking around the seashell island. Aunt Cora pulled out a chair for Kai. In the middle of the counter was a turquoise book called "Secrets of the Sea."

"Are you ready?" Poseidon asked Kai and Delphi. They both gave enthusiastic nods and placed their hands on the book.

Poseidon turned to Captain Hobbs. "Jasper confessed that he framed you all those years ago for breaking the portal. I am truly sorry that I didn't believe you at the time." He pulled a trident necklace out of his pocket. "This should have been yours all along. I want to reinstate you as a Protector." Hobbs happily took it.

Kai, Delphi, and Captain Hobbs all repeated after Poseidon.

I pledge to preserve and protect the sea
And all those creatures that rely on me

I will act kindly and explore with care
I will seek the truth and that which is fair

I will not take what is not given today
I will leave only prints that wash away

No job is too big and no action too small
The care of our sea is a job for us all
In Poseidon's name I pledge

"Welcome back, Hobbs. And a big welcome to you, Kai and Delphi," Poseidon said with a big smile. "You are now officially Poseidon's Protectors! And I have a new mission for you."

HIDDEN PINEAPPLE ANSWER KEY

There are 15 pineapples hidden throughout the illustrations in this story. Did you spot them all?

CHAPTER 1 = 🍍

CHAPTER 2 = 🍍

CHAPTER 3 = NONE

CHAPTER 4 = 🍍

CHAPTER 5 = 🍍

CHAPTER 6 = 🍍

CHAPTER 7 = 🍍

CHAPTER 8 = NONE

CHAPTER 9 = 🍍

CHAPTER 10 = 🍍

CHAPTER 11 = 🍍

CHAPTER 12 = NONE

CHAPTER 13 = 🍍

CHAPTER 14 = 🍍

CHAPTER 15 = NONE

CHAPTER 16 = 🍍

CHAPTER 17 = 🍍

CHAPTER 18 = NONE

CHAPTER 19 = 🍍

CHAPTER 20 = 🍍

Hi!
DID YOU ENJOY THE STORY?
I know I did!

If you want to join the team as we go on more adventures, then leave a review! Otherwise, we won't know if you're up for the next mission. And when we set out on the journey, you may never get to hear about it!

> **YOU CAN LEAVE A REVIEW WHEREVER YOU FOUND THE BOOK.**

The gang and I are excited to see you on the next adventure!
Hopefully there are snacks . . .

ALSO BY MARINA J. BOWMAN

Scaredy Bat

A supernatural detective series for kids with courage, teamwork, and problem solving. If you like solving mysteries and overcoming fears, you'll love this enchanting tale!

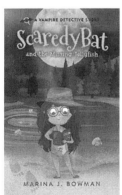

To learn more, visit
scaredybat.com

QUESTIONS FOR DISCUSSION

1. What was your favorite part about this book?
2. What are some of the major themes of this story?
3. Would you rather be able to speak to animals or turn into an animal?
4. If you could create your own Protector Group and Pledge, what would they be?
5. In the story, Kai and Delphi discover that things don't always go as planned. How did they adapt in these situations? When have you had to adapt because things didn't go as planned?
6. The Legend of Pineapple Cove Book #4 ends with some loose ends. If more books come out, what do you think they should be about?

For more Discussion Questions, visit
thelegendofpineapplecove.com/bundle

PIRATE CODE

Create your own secret messages with the
Beetle Island cryptogram!

For more legendary fun, visit
thelegendofpineapplecove.com/bundle

ADD YOUR OWN COLOR TO THE TREASURE ROOM!

ADD YOUR OWN FLAIR TO THE PIRATES OF BEETLE ISLAND!

For more coloring pages, visit
thelegendofpineapplecove.com/bundle

ABOUT THE AUTHOR

MARINA J. BOWMAN is a writer and explorer who travels the world searching for wildly fantastical stories to share with her readers. Ever since she was a child, she has been fascinated with uncovering long lost secrets and chasing the mythical, magical, and supernatural. For her current story, Marina is investigating Pineapple Cove, a mysterious island located somewhere in the Atlantic.

Marina enjoys sailing, flying, and nearly all other forms of transportation. She never strays far from the ocean for long, as it brings her both inspiration and peace. She stays away from the spotlight to maintain privacy and ensure the more unpleasant secrets she uncovers don't catch up with her.

As a matter of survival, Marina nearly always communicates with the public through her representative, Devin Cowick. Ms. Cowick is an entrepreneur who shares Marina's passion for travel and creative storytelling and is the co-founder of Code Pineapple.

Marina's last name is pronounced baʊmən, and rhymes with "now then."